What people are say

"The Interconnecte
strengthen your p
choices, including a [illegible] vegan. Being vegan is not about deprivation. Through its intriguing chapters, this book authenticates that vegan means affirmation of all good things that benefit the earth, other animals, and millions of people who are suffering. The Interconnectedness of Life is a treasure trove filled with stories and ideas for growth and joy that stand ready for revelation and affirmative action. If you are already vegan or have friends and family on the verge or in need of a nudge, Michael's book is for you and for them."
– Karen Davis, PhD, Author and President of United Poultry Concerns

"I loved the book! I thought it was well done and factual. Great job! You obviously put a lot of time and thought into writing it. I enjoyed your writing skills and am honored to have gotten to be one of the first to read it."
– Victoria Everett aka Crazy Banana Lady

"I really like the book that Michael put together. I was even delighted that he called out the "junk-food" veganism. It is nice to see Michael tackle this topic with a raw realism that forces you to pay attention. Whether you love or hate it, you will take away something of benefit from the book."
– Vaughn Berkeley, MBA, President of CM Berkeley Media Group

"If we as humans are ever to break free from the path of destruction we currently find ourselves on, it is crucial that we as a species embrace the concept of nonviolence. Michael's message is clear, love is the glue that connects everything to everything else, and denial of this has led to wide-scale suffering for countless animals, planet-wide. If we are ever to bring this planet back from the brink of seemingly inevitable despair, we must recognize animals as our brethren and realize we are here to guide and protect them, not to abuse, slaughter

and gluttonously devour them, as has sadly been the case since the dawning of recorded history. The Interconnectedness of Life goes far in explaining just why we need to step back and take a look at our relationship with other earthlings, and sheds light on the daily, forced atrocities animals must endure before finally ending butchered sizzled and fried on our dinner tables."
– Mango Wodzak, Author of Destination Eden

"The very essence of Interconnectedness of Life is in the name itself. The author has penned concerns, emotions, and change all in a heartwarming, heartbreaking, yet uplifting book. His words are powerful and bittersweet articulating reality. A must read for all. Change is here!"
– Dr. Ma Maha-Atma, Msc.D., Prema Bhakti Yogani

"I've known Michael for a few years and he has impressed me as a kind-hearted person who is sincere in his passion for animals and desire to help people. I read Michael's book and it was a great job. I am delighted to highly recommend The Interconnectedness of Life to readers who want to learn more about veganism."
– Jenny Berkeley, RN, CHN, Author and Co-Publisher of EternityWatch Magazine

"This book is a masterpiece of information on veganism. The arguments are explained in a simple and deep meaningful way allowing the reader to acknowledge the universal kindness and love for all sentient beings."
– Luciana Milia, Founder of www.ionontimangio.com

"Reading the Interconnectedness of Life, you feel as though you are sitting with Michael himself as he opens his heart and tells his story of vegan awakening. In this genuine and heartfelt book, he covers all the reasons why human beings must end the exploitation and killing of animals if life on earth is to survive. What I love the most about Michael's work, though, is that he goes to the heart of the solution for us all. He makes it clear that our task "to create peace and heaven on

earth" requires the raising of human consciousness to the highest level of unconditional love for all life. This book will help many people become vegan, and thus help bring peace, freedom and love to all beings."
– Judy Carman, MA, Author of Peace to all Beings and The Missing Peace

"The Interconnectedness of Life articulates in an uplifting and engaging way the many correspondences between vegan living and building a healthier world. Michael Lanfield weaves stories from his personal journey of transformation together with the latest research on nutrition and ecology. To this, he adds a judicious selection of wise words from sages of many times and places. The result is a literary banquet that is sure to inspire and guide readers to greater compassion, clarity, health, and understanding. Highly recommended."
– Dr. Will Tuttle, Author of the #1 Amazon bestselling book The World Peace Diet

"Complete – If I had to describe The Interconnectedness of Life with one word, that is the one I would choose. Michael has poured his soul into this book, and as an author myself I can attest to the time and effort that it takes to write a quality book. Michael has written a book that covers every facet of veganism. This book goes further than covering just the environmental, health, and ethical reasons for living a vegan lifestyle; in addition to those three well discussed pillars of veganism Michael covers other topics such as the spirituality of veganism, human rights, and even fruitarianism, a section that I particularly enjoyed. Michael breaks veganism down into its simplest form, and covers every aspect you could think of – and some that you didn't. Not only does this book clearly explain every aspect of veganism, but it ties and connects them together. This book *is* Interconnectedness."
– Jon Kozak, Raw Food Lifestyle Coach, Personal Trainer, and Author of Nuts About No Nuts

The Interconnectedness of Life

Michael Lanfield

Foreword by Karen Davis, PhD
Author and President of United Poultry Concerns

We Are Interconnected Films
2014

2015 Newly Revised Edition

ISBN-13: 978-1502892195 **ISBN-10:** 1502892197

Foreword: Karen Davis, PhD, www.upc-online.org
Cover Drawings: Raffaella Cosco, www.raffaellacosco.com
Title Design: Michael Lanfield, www.michaellanfield.com

Published by:
We Are Interconnected Films. Toronto, Canada.
http://www.weareinterconnected.com

Thank you to the following people for the support: John Mekdeci, Susan Endlich, Viktor Turcsik, Tara Gardner, Aldona Egiert, David Shafir, Rosemary Waigh, Emily Middin, Tushar Mehta, Josephine Later, Andrei Popescu, Diane Gandee Sorbi, Rana Ta, Kimiko Yamamoto, Emily Abu-middin, Barbara Lamb, Jenny and Vaughn Berkeley from EternityWatch Magazine and all the supporters and followers on social media and elsewhere.

DEDICATION

I want to thank everyone who has helped make this project possible. I would also like to congratulate those of you who picked up this book and started reading it. It would make me very happy if you find even one point useful and apply it to your lives.

I have many inspirations, but most of all, I would especially like to show my utmost appreciation for and love to Dr. Will Tuttle for creating an excellent read, probably the greatest book on the face of the earth, The World Peace Diet. His book, lectures, videos, interviews and music have inspired me to write my own book, The Interconnectedness of Life, which you are about to read.

Another book that really inspired me and changed my life tremendously is Destination Eden by Mango Wodzak. I encourage everyone to pick up these two books right away.

My deepest gratitude also goes to my mother, for being there for me all these years. If it weren't for her, this book would probably never have been written.

And my last - but not least - word, goes out to all animals; my love and empathy goes out to each and every one of you imprisoned and slaughtered for human greed.

I can't possibly forget to thank my good friend James Smart, for his wonderful idea of adding stories from other like-minded individuals, which you will read in Chapter Twenty, Stories of Compassion.

Michael Lanfield

TABLE OF CONTENTS

FOREWORD

Hidden in Plain Sight
By Karen Davis, PhD

Teaching English at the University of Maryland some years ago I launched a magazine of student writings called Impetus. Two autobiographical essays, in particular, are etched in my memory. "My Last Visit to the Circus" describes a child's delight in the circus as – "a fantasyland come true to me." The story, told by Wai Lee, is of a fantasyland transformed to a horror show that she, as a child of seven, stumbles upon by accident. Though she misses seeing the miserable life of elephants and tigers chained together but out of sight, she catches a traumatizing glimpse of meanness and squalor in one of the tents, just feet away from the glamour. Explaining her feelings of shock and betrayal, she writes that for her, "The circus was no longer a paradise; it was a nightmare."

"Crossing the Line" is about a 13-year-old boy's confrontation with a challenge he's been dreading for weeks. "For generations," Brian Kehoe writes, "it had been a tradition on my father's side of the family to take the male children on their first hunting trip when they reached the age of thirteen." He describes the anguish he felt at the thought of having to aim a gun at an animal mixed with his fear of disappointing his father if he refused to kill.

When the dreaded moment comes, at his father's behest, Brian aims his rifle at a large, brown rabbit. In a split-second decision, in a turmoil of emotions, instead of hitting the rabbit, he misses, and the rabbit runs into the woods. On their way home that evening his father hits another rabbit with his jeep and keeps driving, but Brian, seeing the wounded rabbit on the road and perceiving that "his eyes were still full of life," screams at his father, "Stop the jeep! Stop it! He's still alive." The boy jumps out of the moving jeep and looks down: "The rabbit was there, lying on its side, its back broken. I stared in horror as it pawed weakly at the air with all four feet. Its eyes were wide with terror and agony." Brian mercifully kills the rabbit and heads back to the jeep, "crying my brains out," he wrote.

A transformative moment in our lives is when a romantic, idyllic, pleasurable occasion that we have loved or taken for granted as good, normal and necessary is revealed as ugly, needless, brutal and bad. Another inimitable moment is when something that we dread and know to be wrong puts us to the test: Will we succumb to the pressure to do a bad act in order to please our friends, family and community? Will we conform to a pattern cut out for us by others in order to avoid the hassle of social conflict? When the moment to decide arrives, will we rebel against convention and take our stand?

Growing up in a Pennsylvania town I went happily to the circus with my family, never dreaming that the costumed elephants, balancing on their heads, were a scene of profound animal cruelty, degradation, and misery. Even less aware was I then that the hotdogs I ate at the circus, and at picnics, were made out of animals, and that a hotdog – like the circus itself and the typical daily dinner plate – is a form of hell hidden in plain sight. Later, joining the animal rights movement, I discovered many atrocities behind the scenes that required me to make radical changes in my life.

As far back as I can remember I have always loved birds, dogs, rabbits and all animals. I have always hated the suffering of a helpless creature. When our neighbor's pet duck was hit by a car in front of our house, I literally became sick over it. Learning about the Nazi concentration camps and Stalin's death camps while in college, I became so ill that I dropped out of school. A few years later I naively visited the Gulf of St. Lawrence to see the newborn harp seals on the ice with their mothers, only to encounter seal clubbing. So terrible was the experience that, for ten years, I stayed away from any hint of animals being tortured by humans.

But compassion without courage doesn't count. To count, we have to do something about what we learn and how we feel about it. We have to say "No" to the circus and to shooting a pigeon or a rabbit to please our dad. We have to reject a system that says “God” is against gay marriage and racial mingling, single mothers and showing other creatures the love and respect that all beings with feelings deserve. We have to stop treating the natural world like our personal garbage disposal. We have to put life-affirming decisions and loving gestures in place of hurtful and destructive ones, once we become aware and realize that we care.

The Interconnectedness of Life, by Michael Lanfield, which you are about to read, will strengthen your resolve to make brave choices, including a decision to be and remain vegan. Increasingly, we are learning that being vegan will benefit the earth, other animals, and millions of people who are starving and sick, in part because their land is being used for purposes that our species needs to shun if we truly cherish life and our planet. The Interconnectedness of Life offers opportunities for growth and joy that stand ready for revelation, sharing and affirmative action. Let there be change and let it begin with me. Now is the perfect moment to take a Giant Step.

– Karen Davis, PhD, Author and President of *United Poultry Concerns*
United Poultry Concerns is a non-profit organization that promotes the compassionate and respectful treatment of domestic fowl and includes a sanctuary for chickens in Virginia. www.upc-online.org

PREFACE

It has taken me five years to write this book. As I type this introduction, thoughts and ideas whirl chaotically through my mind. How can I explain the experiences and motivations which have given birth to this book? Even now, it is difficult to explain the world I envision for the future. How can I describe my life experiences? Will anyone even take me seriously?

The stories, ideas and facts outlined in this book come from years of experience and scientific research. My hope is to utilize them to enlighten you and to let you understand why non-human animals play such an important role in the survival of this planet. Without them, we probably wouldn't be alive today.

Wouldn't it be nice if we all lived in a peaceful world, with no fear of crime or theft? There would be no locks, keys or security systems. Wouldn't it be nice if there were no world hunger, wars or terrorism? How about bountiful sources of free energy, fresh food and clean water for everyone? A world like this is entirely possible.

I am not talking about a fantasy world or a fairy-tale filled with nonsense. This is a proposal, a set of steps that each one of us can take, to attain a world filled with abundance, love, and peace. For this to happen, we need to step away from the mainstream way of thinking and apply new principles to our lives. If we really want to live in peace we need to think radically (compared to the rest of society). You see, the reason why we are in such a mess is that we live in a materialistic, destructive, money-grubbing society where self-centredness prevails.

Understanding the extent of our problems and acting upon them are the first steps to freeing ourselves. We can then teach others these same principles. These are ancient teachings which are obtainable within us all.

Early on in the writing of this book, I decided not only to include my story of awakening, but others' as well. As a result, biologists, philosophers, authors and activists who have taken the leap toward a vegan lifestyle will also be sharing their stories in Chapter Twenty.

I sincerely hope that you take at least one idea from of this book and apply it to your life, but simply the fact that you read it will mean a lot. Even if you discredit the book in its entirety, or think of it as 'wishy-washy,' as long as you read it with an open mind and absorb all the presented ideas (apply them at your own leisure), I will be happy.

My aim is not to win anyone over. I am just here to enlighten readers to the idea that life can indeed be different. We can live in an Eden-like paradise if we really want to. Again, I am not writing about a fairy-tale or a fantasy world; we can live in a real world that is truly free of violence and suffering, but only if we truly want it and only if we're willing to help it get there.

There is living proof of this. In Chapter Twenty, Stories of Awakening, there are true stories from the lives of several great people: biologist and author Jonathan Balcombe, activist and author of Peace to all Beings and The Missing Peace Judy Carman, activists Diane Gandee Sorbi and Laura Lee and many more! To me, these are the great people that have done something to make the world a better place. Not only are they amazing, each are living proof that every one of us can "be the change they want to see in the world" as Mahatma Gandhi has said.

I don't claim to be an expert on anything; I acquire my knowledge by reading books and Internet articles, by watching documentaries and by learning to understand Mother Earth and the lessons she provides me. I try to prove every fact true before I share it and write down my thoughts as clearly as possible. Of course, website addresses and references change from time to time and it is not always possible to verify each source, but I will try to update the references as the corrections come to my attention.

In the event, that there is a discrepancy with any of the following information it can be addressed by contacting me through my website. It is my intent to make sure that all the work contained here has been properly researched and carefully verified.

Regardless of your age or religious or non-religious affiliation, anyone can understand the ideas outlined in this book and apply them to their lives. After five years of research, writing and soul-searching, it is with pleasure that I offer you The Interconnectedness of Life. Read on my friend…

CHAPTER ONE
HOW LIFE STARTED

The interconnectedness of all life is simply this: realizing that we are interconnected with one another and that we depend on one another for survival. We must love one another unconditionally in order to survive. Love includes not only humans, but all beings. No one is ever excluded, as unconditional love means, by definition, that there are no conditions when it comes to whom or what we love. When we love humans, we must also love animals and nature, or our love is not truly *unconditional.*

First and foremost, let's address the problem that originally disrupted this universal love: the herding culture. It began about ten thousand years ago in what was then known as the Fertile Crescent of the Middle East (what is known today as the country of Iraq), and it spread its way across the world in a very short time.[1-3] Prior to this, humans seem to have been compassionate, loving beings who were nurturing and giving to the earth. We also worked with the earth, foraging for fruit and other edible plants. The emergence of herding habits was considered a remarkable breakthrough in civilization, but ultimately it led to the destruction of the planet.

Ever since the herding revolution we have been programmed to believe that we are part of a hierarchy in which humans are the top species, dominating other living beings and destroying the natural world around us. This has greatly shifted our way of thinking from what it once was.

Anthropologists have come to the conclusion that early humans were mainly plant-eaters, with a large part of their diet consisting of fruit.[4] Since humans came forth from the tropics of Africa, it was natural for us to pick sweet, ripe, delicious fruit along with vegetables, tubers, nuts and seeds in small quantities.

When humans started living in colder climates, they were most likely in search of different types of food that grew in those areas. This was when they started eating flesh, but only to survive, since plant food became scarcer and harder to find. However, the amount of animal food in the diet of these ancestors was still relatively small compared to what we eat today. Today, animal and junk food dominate our diet, and only about five percent of it consists of fresh fruits and vegetables.[5] Most likely, for our ancestors, these numbers would have been switched.

Hunters or Gatherers: The Subsistence Lifestyle

No one knows if we were more of a hunter or gatherer type of society. Anthropologists and paleoanthropologists surveying facial bone structure, have discovered that early humans (hominoids) were mostly fruit eaters and gatherers more than hunters.[6]

> "Man's structure, internal and external compared with that of the other animals, shows that fruit and succulent vegetables are his natural food."[7]
> **Carolus Linnaeus**

> "And what food makes up the bulk of baboon diet? Fruit, of course; so for most of their history, humans were fruitarians."[7]
> **Rynn Berry**

> "All available scientific evidence indicates that humans are frugivorous apes. Regardless of how large and arrogant our cultural egos are, and regardless of unsupportable religious dogma created by ignorant people who knew absolutely nothing of biochemistry, comparative anatomy, genetics, or science thousands of years ago, our physiology is that of a frugivorous ape."[7]
> **Laurie Forti**

"The knowledge we gain from anatomy tells us in no uncertain language that by nature we were intended to be frugivorous and to live on flesh foods violates the fundamental laws of our being... Flesh eating is the antithesis of love. We must work for the abolition of the slaughterhouses, those chambers of horror where so much unnecessary cruelty is enacted. We must try and liberate mankind from the chains that bind him so heavily and so forcibly to the fleshpots of Egypt, and lessen the appalling burden that rests on the shoulders of the creatures, our younger brothers, whom we forget are our younger brothers and fail to treat with brotherly love."[8]

Gordon Latto (22nd World Vegetarian Congress 1973, Ronneby Brunn, Sweden).

Even if we were the hunters that we all claim to be, back then we did not have the tools or weaponry to kill prey let alone tear into their flesh. The earliest recorded weaponry use is the bow and arrow and spear, invented around thirty thousand years ago.[9] In today's modern world, we do not live a subsistence or scavenger type lifestyle. Hunters justify their practice by relating their actions to early humans, who were part of hunter-gatherer, indigenous type society. However, today, a lot of indigenous people rely on grocery stores and shopping centres to meet all their lifestyle needs, with the exception of a few, small ethnic groups around the world who still live by relying on the earth and animals to provide food.

Hunters, like many omnivores, justify their practices by saying it is a more sustainable way of living compared to modern-day factory farming. Even though, it is (admittedly) less violent and more sustainable compared to factory farming, it is by no means our natural and intended lifestyle. Humans are not meant to be killing machines as we are depicted on TV, in movies and in video games. We are meant to be compassionate beings, loving and nurturing to the earth.

No one really knows why we, as a species, initially migrated north. It may have been in search of food when food was scarce. What we know is that when we migrated north, plants became even scarcer. We relied on alpine and other tuber plants that grew north of the tropics; we lived a subsistence lifestyle and ate anything we could find. We could consider ourselves scavengers. It was possibly the only time when this lifestyle may have been considered acceptable, or at least less terrible.

Anytime we kill wildlife there are consequences to our actions. It is a bad act in itself to kill any living creature. When we kill just one animal in nature, we risk disrupting their family. We might kill a mother that has babies. How will those babies fend for themselves out in the wild? Unfortunately, those orphaned animals will eventually die. It is understandable that people living subsistence lifestyles kill animals in order to survive or to feed their village, but we are not living a subsistence lifestyle. When we kill just one animal, we might actually be killing the whole family.

Hunters that kill for recreational sport are still committing violence, which is totally unnecessary for survival. Hunting, in this case, is a bloodshed sport. Other bloodshed sports include coursing, cockfighting, and dog fighting, all which kill large numbers each year. In the US alone, hunters are responsible for the deaths of over 200 million animals every year.[10]

On top of this, animal protein is a foreign protein that our bodies cannot digest.[11] Wild animals, even though they are not factory farmed, still contain fat, cholesterol and naturally occurring hormones which are toxic to our immune system.

Human Physiology

We are not carnivores or even omnivores by nature. Even though we can consume both plants and animals, we are not biologically designed to do so. Our saliva is alkaline and contains a special enzyme that is necessary to pre-digest plant food (and plant food only). Carnivorous animals have acidic saliva and their stomachs produce large amounts of hydrochloric acid, which is necessary to digest flesh. They have a short intestine for quick release of these acidic foods. We have long intestines, therefore eating animal food causes havoc to our bodies. Animal food putrefies for days in our colon. This often leads to constipation.[11]

Also, humans do not have sharp claws or big mouths, let alone fangs, to cut into raw flesh. Our teeth are not sharp like true canine teeth; we have flat molars and small mouths for grinding plants. The largest animals on earth, such as buffalos, giraffes and elephants are natural herbivores; they eat grasses, leaves, and other plant foods and they have teeth like ours. Humans are not meant to eat animal-based food. We could never jump on an animal and bite into his or her flesh or drink from her teat. It is absurd to even think about it.

> "We see that human beings have the gastrointestinal tract structure of a "committed" herbivore. Humankind does not show the mixed structural features one expects and finds in anatomical omnivores such as bears and raccoons. Thus, from comparing the gastrointestinal tract of humans to that of carnivores, herbivores and omnivores we must conclude that humankind's GI tract is designed for a purely plant-food diet."[12]
> **Milton R. Mills, MD**

Infectious Diseases

People are brainwashed into believing that diseases are man-made in scientific laboratories. However, this is not true according to research done by many doctors and scientists, including Michael Greger, MD. Three-quarters of the known diseases of our time have come from eating animals, according to The Humane Society of the United States (HSUS).[13]

In his latest book, *Bird Flu*, Michael Greger points out, "The chief of virology at Hong Kong's Queen Mary Hospital believes that "the cause and solution [of H5N1] lies within the poultry industry."[14]

> "The scientists who unsuccessfully tried to infect human volunteers with wild duck viruses

in the lab even tried passing the virus from one person to the next to enhance human infectivity. They squirted a million infectious doses up the first person's nose, then inoculated a second person with the first person's mucus, and continued down the line. Despite the high doses used and five person-to-person passages, the virus still could not grab hold. A study published in 2006 in *Clinical Infectious Diseases* found that pig farmers are up to 35 times more likely to show evidence of swine flu exposure than those with no occupational contact with pigs, but studies of Canadian wildlife personnel have consistently found them negative for waterfowl virus infection. Although one duck hunter and a few wildlife professionals tested in Iowa showed evidence of exposure to wild bird viruses, influenza viruses found in their natural undisturbed state do not seem to pose a human threat."[15]

"As long as there is poultry, there will be pandemics."[16]
Michael Greger, MD, Physician, Author and Speaker

The vice-president of the European Parliament's Environment Committee said in a press release,

"Factory farming and global transportation are behind the breeding and spreading of diseases like avian influenza. The EU must act now to prevent further outbreaks of such diseases. Measures must be taken to regionalize production, reduce transport distances, and impose animal welfare standards so that European factory farming is phased out in the coming years."[17]

When animals are raised in close proximity to one another, as in factory farming operations, there is a larger breeding ground for infectious diseases to emerge, including influenza. It is highly unlikely for influenza to spread from one bird to another in backyards or wild flocks.[18]

When we domesticated:[19]

Cows and Sheep
We got human *measles*
Which came from *rinderpest virus*

Camels
We got *smallpox*
Which came from *camelpox*

Pigs
We got *whooping cough* (or pertussis)

Chickens
We got *typhoid fever*

Ducks
We got *influenza* (aka the flu)

Water Buffalo
We got *leprosy* (aka Hansen's disease)

Horses
We got the *common cold*

CHAPTER TWO
ENVIRONMENTAL DESTRUCTION

"The environment is interconnected with us: we are constantly taking in oxygen from the atmosphere that is produced from other living things and releasing carbon dioxide that is consumed by other living things; we drink water that has come from fresh water sources in our environment and consume food that comes from other living things, and then excrete waste back into the environment which then becomes food for other creatures; etc. It is important to realize this interconnectedness[...]"[1]
Tracey Hamilton

The Wrong Direction

We are told by governments and city officials to conserve energy and water by changing our showerheads and using low-flow toilets and to drive hybrid automobiles. Is that the proper solution? While these are great things to do, conservation is not the answer. That is, it is not the only answer. We must understand that animal agriculture, in any form, is very resource-intense. Many studies have shown that switching to a plant-based diet will help with our fight against climate change and other environmental problems as well.[2]

Climate Change

According to the United Nations Food and Agricultural Organization report from 2006, Livestock's Long Shadow, eighteen percent of annual greenhouse gas emissions are attributed to raising livestock.[3] Another analysis, by World Watch Institute in 2009, reported that at least fifty-one percent of all carbon emissions are attributed to livestock and their by-products. That is more than all forms of transportation combined.[4]

A highly recommended book on animal agriculture's negative impact is Supreme Master Ching Hai's, From Crises to Peace: The Organic Vegan Way is the Answer.[5] According to the vegan, international, non-profit channel, Supreme Master Television, eighty percent of global warming could be stopped if we all switched to a vegan diet.[6]

Farmed animals' excrements, flatulence, belching and breathing also contribute to climate change by emitting methane into the air and into our waterways.[7] Feedlots and factory farms manage the animals' wastes by diverting them into huge open cesspools they euphemistically call lagoons. These huge lagoons pollute our environment, and sometimes spill into nearby lakes, rivers and streams, killing millions of fish, birds, and other animals.[8]

Some believe that by eating 'local' it will help to cut down on these problems and help to reduce the amount of animal waste and destruction caused by raising them. According to a report by the World Preservation Foundation, however, "A vegan diet reduces emissions seven times more than local eating."[9] This means even local eating cannot do as much as going completely vegan can.

In order to produce animal food, we first need to feed and raise animals, transport them to the slaughterhouses, slaughter them, freeze and transport them to the supermarkets. And do not forget about all the lights, fans and other resources that are required in intensified animal agriculture.

> "A substantial reduction of impacts would only be possible with a substantial worldwide diet change, away from animal products."[10]
> **United Nations Environmental Programme**

Deforestation

Approximately one to one and a half acres of forests around the world are cut down every second so humans can gorge on animal food. This is to grow food for farmed animals and for livestock that are grazing. A vegan saves, on average, one acre of trees per year.[11] In the past two hundred years, according to some reports, as much as seventy percent – or more! – of forests worldwide have been cleared.[12]

Water

Raising animals for food is also a severe waste of water. About one percent of the world's fresh water is usable, and seventy percent of this fresh water is diverted for animal agriculture.[13] According to World Watch Institute, twenty-three percent of our global water is used for agriculture.[14] In fact, it takes more water to produce a pound of steak or a glass of milk than it does to produce potatoes.

> David Pimentel explains:
> "The data we had indicated that a beef animal consumed 100 kg of hay and 4 kg of grain per 1 kg of beef produced. Using the basic rule that it takes about 1,000 litres of water to produce 1 kg of hay and grain, thus about 100,000 litres are required to produce 1 kg of beef."[15]

Land

World Watch Institute found that twenty-six percent of land worldwide is used for grazing livestock, and thirty-three percent is used for growing crops to feed livestock.[16] The Food and Agriculture Organization of the United Nations, *Long Shadow*, reports that, "A massive 70% of all agricultural land – is used for rearing farmed animals." Since 1970, more than ninety percent of the Amazonian rainforest itself has begun to be used for livestock pasture.[17]

> Dr. Douglas Graham, author of *The 80/10/10 Diet*, claims that
> "Using fruits and vegetables as our main food source, we can actually produce 100 times more food per acre than we can on a standard Western diet. We can feed 100 times as many people or feed the people we have now on 1/100th the amount of land, freeing out fantastic

land and energy for recreation and other healthful pursuits."[18]

Other Catastrophes

A vegan diet can reduce or maybe even stop other environmental catastrophes as well. Because of our addiction to animal food we are losing topsoil at an alarming rate. In the Southern US, cattle grazing is causing the land to become desert-like. Droughts, erosion, and other climatic devastations are becoming common. Nature is not responsible for this, we are.

According to a 2006 report by the Livestock, Environment and Development Initiative of the Food and Agriculture Organization of the United Nations, "The livestock industry is one of the largest contributors to environmental degradation worldwide."[19]

CHAPTER THREE
HEALTH IMPLICATIONS

"Diets are not something to be followed for days, weeks, or months. They should form the basis of everyday food choices for the rest of one's life."[1]
Michael Greger, MD, Physician, Author and Speaker

After reading the book *Destination Eden* by Mango Wodzak[2] and after years of self-teaching and reading hundreds of other books, magazines, and Internet articles on nutrition and health, I have come to the conclusion that nutritional science is not so important as we may think it is. In reality, there are so many conflicting theories and scientific studies that I have lost faith even in most true science.

We all know from textbooks, and from our parents, that fruit and vegetables (in their natural state of course – that is raw, unheated and untouched) are the healthiest foods available to us. This means, of course, that we must consume succulent vegetables (such as leafy greens) and sweet fruit before any other food.

We know that sugary foods are what our palates go for, and sweet fruit is perfect for that. Of course, eating only fruit seems bizarre to most of us, as we are not brought up to eat just fruit and fruit alone. I highly recommend reading Mango Wodzak's book, *Destination Eden,* which talks about this.[2] Even though I do not look at nutrition in-depth like I once did, I still offer nutritional information, comparing a standard Western diet (high in animal flesh, dairy, and eggs) with a vegan and fruit based diet.

In practical terms, we do not need to count calories or have a deep understanding of the nutrients in food, but it is just as well to have this knowledge when starting out. When we progress our diet to veganism, and then to raw food, and then to fruitarianism, nutrition is not very important. As long as we eat unprocessed, low-fat, whole plant food, overall we will be doing great.

We know from the earlier chapter that an animal-based diet is very destructive to the environment, destroying not only the nature around us, but the homes of millions of creatures living in the wild. It destroys not only the environment, but also our own health.

GMOs (Genetically Modified Organisms)

In today's society, certain foods are genetically modified. In Canada, corn, soy, canola oil and sugar beets are genetically modified.[3] Unfortunately, many other foods contain one or more of these ingredients. In North America, food containing GMO ingredients are not required to be labelled, so we do not know what we are eating or feeding to our children.[4] If you have any concerns about what is a genetically modified food and what is not, purchase organic when possible. Organic produce is not genetically modified.

You may think this is the worst we have to deal with, but that is not true. Even though GMO's and chemicals are a rampant problem there is an even bigger problem when it comes to our health, as you are about to read below.

The Problem with Animal Food

It is scientifically proven that animal food, even produced organically or caught in the wild, are the leading cause of most Western diseases and ailments.[5] Even if you eat fruit and vegetables laden with chemicals and pesticides, an enzyme in your body called mixed-function oxidase (MFO) will inactivate the chemicals and form healthy cells.[6] As a result, even conventionally-grown fruit and vegetables are healthier than animal products.

This does not mean we should skip out on organic produce just because our bodies can cope with the pesticides and chemicals. Not only may conventionally grown produce be genetically modified, it may also contain fewer nutrients than organic produce, and farmers are exposed to the chemicals and pesticides that are sprayed on the crops. Purchasing organics also ensures that employees are safe from pesticides and that chemicals do not poison the environment. There are hundreds, if not thousands of scientific studies proving that a meat-based diet cause more chronic disease than any other diet or life factor. A meat-based diet raises the risk for certain cancers, heart disease, kidney issues, obesity, diabetes, autoimmune diseases and food-borne illnesses.[7]

There are many reasons for this: first, when animal flesh is cooked, it forms cancer-causing carcinogens called heterocyclic amines or HCA's. This goes for all red and white meat, chicken and fish. Vegetables do not form heterocyclic amines while cooking.[8]

Secondly, the bad cholesterol (called LDL cholesterol or low-density lipoprotein) which is only present in animal food, contributes to atherosclerosis, which leads to heart disease.[9]

While cholesterol is important for a fully functioning immune system, our bodies naturally produce it at the levels we need.[10]

Animal food is a definite problem for our bodies. Animal products contribute to the breakdown of our immune system and lead to faster aging.[11] This is why vegans live, on average, fifteen years longer than meat eaters.[12]

> "Even small amounts of animal-based foods in rural China raised the risk for Western diseases."[13]
>
> **Dr. T. Colin Campbell, Author of *The China Study***

Protein

Another issue with meat consumption is the vast amount of protein it adds into the typical Western diet. It has been shown that the average Western diet has sixteen percent of its calories from protein.[14] This amount can impair the kidneys, leach calcium, zinc, vitamin B, iron and magnesium from the body, and cause osteoporosis, heart disease, cancer and obesity.[15] One reason is that when we consume animal protein, which is too acidic for our body to handle, the acidity must be neutralized. Calcium phosphate is taken from the bones and then calcium leaves through urination. This process leads to brittle bones or osteoporosis.[16]

The average human needs much less protein than we are led to believe. According to Dr. Douglas Graham, the author of The 80/10/10 Diet, ten percent of our total calories from protein is all we need. The same applies to pregnant or lactating women, infants, children, elders, athletes, and bodybuilders. Fruit and vegetables contain a significant amount of protein.[17] Even T. Colin Campbell, the author of The China Study, recommended the ratio 80/10/10 to be the healthiest diet.[18]

The World Health Organization (WHO) stated a minimum of 2.5 percent of our total calories from protein is required for the average human. The safe level was set at five percent.[19] This means that eating a variety of whole plant food will meet, or even exceed, the World Health Organization's standards.

> "On a diet of fruits and vegetables only, it is likely that your total protein intake will average about 5% of calories or slightly higher."[20]
> **Dr. Douglas Graham, Author of *The 80/10/10 Diet***

Even a small amount of animal protein is known to leach calcium from the bones. This is why people with the highest animal product consumption (like the Inuit) have the highest rates of osteoporosis on the planet.[21]

> According to Tim Van Orden,
> "The body doesn't efficiently break down protein we eat; it synthesizes it from the amino acids. Amino acids are building blocks of life, which help build muscle. All amino acids are derived from fresh fruits and vegetables."[22]

"There is no doubt that the consumption of animal protein and fats is linked to the formation of cancer, heart disease, diabetes, autoimmune diseases, of which there are a multitude: multiple sclerosis, Parkinson's disease, arthritis, dementia and Alzheimer's disease. In fact most, if not all the diseases that affect modern society today can be linked to animal proteins and fats."[23]

Dr. T. Colin Campbell, Author of *The China Study*

"Eating animal products has killed more people over the last century than all the car accidents, all the wars and all the natural disasters combined."[24]

Dr. Neal Barnard, Author and *President of Physicians Committee for Responsible Medicine*

Fat

Fat, in high quantities, is very harmful to our bodies, whether it comes from animal or plant sources. Too much fat in our blood leads to increased chances of Western-type diseases. But how much fat is adequate?

According to various doctors, nutritionists and health experts, around ten percent or less of our total calories should come from fats.[25] Even if we were to eat nothing but raw fruit and vegetables with no overt fats, one would average three to five percent fat from their total calories. Adding a few nuts and seeds to the diet still increases the fat intake to only ten percent or less.[26]

There are good and bad fats of course, but if one is eating fruit and vegetables (in their natural state, raw) as one's primary calorie source; one would not have to worry about bad fats. Bad fats are the ones that lead to health problems and weight gain. Good fats are called omega-3 fatty acids.

Omega-3s

Fish are synonymous with omega-3 content and are touted as a health food.[27] Fish, however, are also contaminated with dioxins, polychlorinated biphenyls (PCBs), toxic heavy metals from industrial wastes (such as mercury, lead, cadmium, and arsenic), and other residues from mining and industrial production, as well as noxious pharmaceutical residues and radioactive contamination from nuclear leakage.[28]

When fish are frozen, their omega-3 content starts to break down. This releases free radicals, which lead to a wide variety of diseases.[29, 30] Omega-3 can be obtained without cholesterol, fat and animal protein in flax seeds, chia seeds, walnuts, soybeans, tofu, tempeh, dark leafy greens, and seaweeds.[31] Even fruit has small amounts of omega-3s, and eating a variety of fruits while getting enough calories throughout the week will supply your body with sufficient omega-3s to function.

Dairy

The main protein in milk is called casein. Howard F. Lyman, author of *Mad Cowboy,* quotes; "Casein is shown in laboratory tests to promote cancerous cells like pouring gasoline onto a fire."[32] Milk also contains significant amounts of saturated and trans fats which lead to increased cholesterol levels and increased risk for artery blockages and heart problems.[33]

One recent review points out that the following natural chemicals are present in cow's milk: prolactin, somatostatin, melatonin, oxytocin, growth hormone, leuteinizing hormone-releasing hormone, thyrotropin-releasing hormone, thyroid releasing hormone, vasoactive intestinal peptide, calcitonin, parathyroid hormone, corticosteroids, estrogens, progesterone, insulin, epidermal growth factor, insulin-like growth factor, erythropoietin, bombesin, neurotensin, motilin, and cholecystokinin.[34] Not many are aware that milk is also full of blood, puss, and feces.[35, 36]

There is also 50 – 60 mg of cholesterol in a 56.7 g (2 oz.) serving of cheddar or mozzarella cheese. That is as much per gram as in a steak or ground beef.[37] Even low-fat cow's milk contains significant amounts of fat. Based on Cronometer.com calculations, one percent milk contains approximately 20 percent calories from fat, two percent milk contains 35 percent and homogenized (or whole, 3.25 percent) milk contains 47 percent. Cheddar cheese contains approximately 75 percent calories from fat and butter is virtually 100 percent calories from fat.[38]

There is a natural chemical in dairy called casomorphin which is supposed to double the size of the baby calf within the first year of birth. This chemical keeps the calf coming back for more. Casomorphin is a drug; notice *morphine* in the name.[39] This is why most people are addicted to dairy products, especially cheese. They want cheese on a baked potato, cheese on burgers and fries, cheese on everything in sight! You cannot even get a salad without them putting cheese on it. It is ridiculous! Dr. T. Colin Campbell found: "For all of the experiments we used casein, which is 87 percent of cow's milk protein. So the next logical question was whether plant protein has the same effect on cancer promotion as casein. The answer is an astonishing no. In these experiments, plant protein did not promote cancer growth, even at the highest levels of intake."[40]

Eggs

Eggs are one of the highest sources of cholesterol on the planet. Each whole, raw, fresh egg (large 50g) contains 187mg of cholesterol. Eggs also contain significant amounts of fat and animal protein.[41] Eggs are touted as essential for their protein, but even one egg a day increases the risk for Western-type diseases.[42]

> According to dherbs.com, "Eating eggs can promote a host of diseases and pathologies. Eggs can play a pivotal role in some female reproductive diseases including fibroid tumours, uterine cysts, breast cancer and menstrual irregularities. Also, since these chicken eggs are sterilized or infertile, they are in fact impairing their own sexual fertility and

> potency. Eating eggs can certainly change or alter your bio-chemical, genetic, and molecular makeup and make you susceptible to a host of diseases and pathologies. The sterilization process of commercial eggs is used to prevent the eggs from decaying, but it creates health risks for women who consume the sterilized eggs. Everything you eat, whether it is negative or positive, natural or unnatural, affects your entire being. So yes, eggs play a role in infertility and impotence.[43]

Vegan Diet for Health

Unlike an animal-based diet, a vegan diet contains on average more antioxidants, phytochemicals, and anti-aging properties. Plants are the only source of fibre; they are very beneficial to the immune system. Animal food does not contain fibre.[44]

A vegan diet also contains ample amounts of calcium, iron, zinc and omega-3 fatty acids.[45-47] People believe that poor health is associated with old age or is genetically inherited, but this is not the case. It has been shown that most illnesses are associated with diet. Eating a well-balanced, plant-based, vegan diet (mostly raw) can slow down, or even reverse, most, if not all, the diseases that affect modern society today.[48] With the proper diet and exercise (and refraining from smoking and drinking), a person of 80 years can often perform as efficiently as a person of 30.

As well, a diet high in raw fresh fruit and vegetables is a better choice than one primarily of cooked and processed food.

> "Until then, I was like most athletes who believed you needed meat to build muscle. But after my vegan awakening, I became determined to turn that myth upside-down. So I started learning more about nutrition and working hard to make my dream come true.

And here I am today – the world's first champion vegan bodybuilder."[49]

Kenneth G. Williams, Vegan Bodybuilder and Spokesperson

The Vegan Food Guide

I have decided to include a vegan food guide in this book. My recommendations may be slightly different from other sources, but these are just my own recommendations and what has worked for me over the years. Of course, my diet recommendations may change a little over time.

Must-Do

– Eat a 100% vegan diet. No animal products at all.

– Eat a variety of raw fruit and vegetables (including a good portion of tender leafy greens) throughout the week.

– Drink enough water throughout the day so that your urine is clear.

– Consume B_{12} fortified food or take a B_{12} supplement.

– Average at least nine hours of sleep on a daily basis; best to go to bed early and wake up early. Even if we cannot sleep, horizontal rest is important.

– At least one hour of moderate exercise daily.

Optional

– Include a portion of cooked, vegan food in your diet.

– Minimize or exclude the consumption of refined and processed foods.

– Minimize or exclude all caffeinated products including coffee, energy drinks, colas, teas, etc.

– Try to limit or exclude the intake of vegetable oils. Oils (even olive and coconut oils, cold-pressed and organic) are 100 percent-refined fat, empty calories with most nutrients removed.

– Try to limit or exclude the intake of salt.

– Include non-dairy milks such as soy, rice, hemp, oat or almond in your diet. Try purchasing brands that are organic and fortified.

– Some people may need to supplement their diet with vitamin D (D_2) or consume vitamin D fortified food. Be aware that most vitamin D_3 (cholecalciferol) is made from lanolin, a yellow substance secreted by the sebaceous glands "oil" glands of sheep. There is a vegan D_3 version that is derived from lichens.

– Analog (fake) vegan deli meats, burgers, veggie dogs and cheeses are great transitional foods. Make sure they are vegan. Some analog meat products or veggie cheeses may include animal ingredients like casein or whey protein. Check the ingredients or contact the company to make sure.

Going vegan still allows the possibility to cook delicious food. It is possible to bake without eggs or cows milk because there are many excellent alternatives. Analog meats have been suggested for transition only.

CHAPTER FOUR
ANIMAL AGRICULTURE

> "As long as people will shed the blood of innocent creatures, there can be no peace, no liberty, no harmony between people. Slaughter and justice cannot dwell together."[1]
> **Isaac Bashevis Singer, writer and Nobel laureate (1902–1991)**

> "When people understand the gruesome truth behind animal farming and the innocence of all the animals who sacrifice their lives, it is easy to see that eating dead flesh of another being is not only unnecessary, it leaves us with a trail of bloody footprints."[2]
> **Supreme Master Ching Hai, poet, painter, musician, writer, and entrepreneur**

Most animals raised for food in Western countries, live on factory farms. These are extremely filthy places where animals are denied all natural behaviours. Hens lay eggs, broiler chickens supply meat, cows supply everything from dairy to hamburger, veal, and leather, and pigs give us pork.

Every year about seventy billion land animals around the world are slaughtered for consumption.[3] That figure is around seven hundred million in Canada and ten billion in the US.[4, 5] This number does not include the ones who do not make it to slaughter, marine animals such as fish or shrimp, or insects like bees, worms or ants. These animals' lives are cut short when their production level drops or when they are deemed 'unprofitable.' It is a system of utmost cruelty. Organic, you think? It is basically the same system (as will be shown).[6]

Hens

Hens are probably the worst treated animals on the planet. In the US, more than ninety-five percent of all hens raised for eggs are crowded in battery cages.[7] Currently, about sixty percent of all hens worldwide are raised in industrialized systems, most of those being battery cage systems.[8] This means as many as eleven hens may be crammed into one cage. This is actually quite common. Each hen has approximately the size of a notebook on which to stand. The birds are literally standing on one another and can never even lift a wing. It is agonizing for them as everything natural, such as perching or raising a family, is denied to them. As they start to lay eggs, the eggs drop onto a conveyor belt.

The birds, because of over confinement and stress, rub up against the wires of the cages and eventually lose most of their feathers. While this may not seem serious, their feathers are needed to protect their skin from diseases and from extreme temperatures. There are rows of cages (called tiers), and below the cages are manure pits (also called waste pits), which collect the feces, urine, and vomit. These fall from the upper tiers to the lower ones, through rows of cages and onto other hens.

In this form of factory farming, every bird is crammed as tightly as possible, they are fed antibiotics, feathers fly about and there is the constant unbearable stench of ammonia in the air. Most of the hens end up with respiratory issues, eye damage; and some may even go blind.

When in confinement, hens peck at one another because of the lack of space and stressful living conditions. To combat this, the industry debeaks baby hens; that is, factory farm workers cut off half their beak with a hot blade or remove it with an iron. This is extremely painful to the birds. The pain is similar to pulling off a fingernail. The hens' beak is their most sensitive organ, and slicing off the tip is an extremely painful procedure which makes them suffer their whole life until they are slaughtered or discarded. For just about all factory farms, de-beaked birds have difficulty picking up food, and some will even starve from not eating.

When a hen's egg production declines she is violently yanked out of her cage, even if they are caught in the wires of the cage and transported many miles, without food or water to slaughter. Many die during transportation.

As the egg-laying variety does not grow fast enough for the broiler industry, all these male chicks are killed right away. This is done either by crushing them alive in a blender, to be used in pet food or fed back to other birds or throwing them alive into bags to slowly suffocate, or throwing them in bins to die.

Because the egg-laying phase is unpredictable and infrequent and does not maximize profits for the egg farmers, in the US, farmers use a technique called *forced moulting* where the hens are starved for up to twenty-one days in order to force them into another egg-laying cycle.[9]

The documentary ***Fowl Play*** provides more information.[7]

Chickens and Turkeys

Chickens and turkeys raised for meat are genetically altered to grow so large that their legs cannot withstand the weight. Because of this, some of them will succumb to heart attacks and osteoporosis.[10] Chickens and turkeys are raised in large sheds where thousands of them are crammed together.[11] Broiler chicks are sent off to slaughter as little as thirty-five days young, still babies.[12] Normally, in nature, they can live up to fifteen years.[13]

Because of overcrowding, turkeys get their beaks cut off shortly after birth. This excruciating pain makes eating difficult. Sometimes even their toes are cut off, and then walking and even standing are difficult.[14] All their natural behaviours, such as perching, nesting, dust-bathing, foraging, roaming and even flapping their wings are denied, as in the egg industry. They do not have access to the outdoors or to natural light. The sheds they are kept in are so full of ammonia, and the ground so covered with feces and urine, that the birds develop respiratory diseases.[15]

Pigs

Pigs are considered the most intelligent of all farm animals, and are ranked the top five out of all animals.[16] After a few days or weeks piglets are castrated without anaesthetics, supposedly to produce a fattier grade of meat; and to avoid boar taint, which is offensive odour or taste during the cooking or eating of pork.[17, 18] Because of the confinement and stressful living conditions, piglets get their tails, ears and teeth all cut without pain killers. Even then, pigs try to bite one another's tails, and they are driven to becoming cannibals.[19]

In the wild you would never see hogs eating one another or hardly any of these diseases, but in factory and even organic farms it is common to see pigs with bladder ruptures, deformed bladders, deformed bodies, and sores many times their natural size. These farm animals are rarely if ever, looked at or treated by veterinarians because to do so would drive up the production costs.[20]

Professor Stanley Curtis of Pennsylvania State University found that pigs play and excel at joystick-controlled video games. He observed that they are capable of abstract representation and are able to hold an icon in their mind and remember it at a later date. Pigs are extremely intelligent and compassionate, and one even saved a boy from drowning. It is also shown that chickens and other animals mimic what they see on television and learn to distinguish different shapes.[21] Farm animal are smart and deserve our respect.

Cows

Dairy products (such as milk, cheese, butter, and yogurt) come from the secretion of cows. Dairy cows are chained to stalls and live on concrete floors their whole lives; unable to lie down or move around.[22] In order to produce a steady flow of milk, they must be impregnated. This is done by artificially inseminating them, by inserting a steel rod and/or hand in their vagina.[23] Dairy cows are impregnated while simultaneously lactating.[24] Cows are also fed ground up animals, including their own species, so they become cannibals. In the United States and England, cattle have tested positive for mad cow disease because of this feeding of cows to cows.[25]

Dairy cows are hooked up to milking machines several times a day until their milk production declines. This process may lead to infection of the udder called mastitis, often when the cows produce excess milk.[26] After a dairy cows milk declines she is sent to slaughter and made into cheap ground beef.[29] Downers (animals too sick to even stand) are dragged away by chains, or pushed with forklifts.[27, 28]

Steers are branded with a hot iron which causes painful third degree burns. Often their horns are cut off and this causes great nerve pain. Male veal calves are taken from their mothers within a day of birth, chained to stalls that restrict their movement, in order to keep muscles from developing, fed an iron deficient liquid diet to keep flesh pale, and denied bedding, water and light. After four months of this miserable life, they too are slaughtered.[29-31]

The Free Range Myth
Free Range, Free Roaming, and Cage Free

As in battery-caged birds or other factory farmed animals, free range and free roaming facilities still allow animals to be housed in cramped sheds with thousands or tens of thousands of other animals, some literally standing on one another. Debeaking and other mutilations and the inhumane culling of male chicks are still present like in factory farming.

To be certified as free range, facilities must give animals access to the outdoors. But it does not specify the quality or duration of the access. Even five minutes and access to a muddy barren lot in between sheds is sufficient to be labeled as free range. In the end, all animals go to their deaths to the same slaughterhouses as those who were raised on factory farms.[32, 33]

Happy Cows – Humane Milk

This is a falsehood to make customers feel happy about their buying choices believing that cows are happy every step of the way from the farm to their fork. This is far from the truth. Though some cows may be pastured raised as in most cows raised for beef in Australia, it is anything but happy for the cows.

Organic

According to *humanemyth.org*, "organic standards pertain largely to the content of animal feed and the use of medicines put into animals' bodies, rather than how the animals are treated. At many organic farms, antibiotics are withheld from sick animals in order to maintain the saleability of dairy, eggs, or meat that will be labeled "organic." This creates tremendous suffering as the animals are left to either die or recover without the benefit of medicine. Numerous investigations of organic farms have revealed animals living in conditions which are deplorable, yet do not violate "organic standards."[34]

What About Organic, Small Backyard Farmers?

No matter how animals are treated they are still considered production units and when we steal their purposes we lose our purpose. Animals' bodies and their products are not ours to use and consume. They belong to animals. We have no right to be stealing from chickens, cows or any other animal, their products that are intended for them or their babies.

All egg farmers, even organic backyard operations, purchase hens from hatcheries where the males are typically ground up alive because they are of no use to the industry. When animals' production declines they are usually sent to slaughter. Anytime we own animals to be used for profit it is violence.

Transportation and Slaughter

There are very few regulations when it comes to the transportation and slaughter of farm animals. In Canada, farm animals are allowed to be transported in any extreme weather conditions without food, rest or water for up to seventy-two hours and they are slaughtered in a way that maximizes farmers' profits.[35]

Many animals are slaughtered while fully conscious, in a slaughter that can never be considered humane or painless. Line speeds are extremely fast; some animals are even still alive when they go into the scalding tanks.[36] Slaughterhouse workers beat, kick and punch animals to get them to move. Even an owner of a family farm was caught on camera kicking a downed cow to get her to move.[37]

Humane Slaughter

Animals are usually hung upside down by one or two legs, and are stabbed or have their throats slit. This can never be considered humane. According to the Oxford Dictionaries, the definition of *Humane* is, "Having or showing compassion or benevolence".[38]

> "To have one's throat involuntarily slit may be many things, but few on the receiving end of such an act would be likely to call it merciful, or compassionate. Hence, humane slaughter is an oxymoron."[39]
> **Humanemyth.org**

Other Animals

Ducks, geese, horses, and bison are some of the other animals that are raised for food in Canada, the US, and other countries. These animals are delicacies in many cultures, but a lot of people in this country are appalled when they find bison or horse on the menu.

Ducks are used for their flesh and livers and are confined in cages so small that the birds cannot even move around. For foie gras, they have a long pipe or tube shoved down their throats several times daily, pumping them with huge amounts of grains so that they produce a diseased, fatty liver considered a delicacy. The diseased liver grows to about ten times its size in a normal duck.[40]

Antibiotics and Drugs

Why haven't doctors found a cure for the common cold or flu? Why are we continuously using stronger antibiotics and drugs to cure illnesses? Is it because we are injecting all kinds of antibiotics and growth hormones into animals and feeding them food laced with pesticides, fungicides, and other chemicals? Absolutely!

New, stronger strains of diseases are occurring in herds everywhere; therefore, new, stronger antibiotics are needed to treat animals. It is the same with humans; new, stronger antibiotics are needed to treat today's illnesses than were needed in the past. Antibiotics are becoming less effective.

Worldwide, eighty percent of antibiotics are administered to livestock.[41] There are between seven and twenty-one different vaccines that are injected into animals and their feed.[42] Is it any wonder we get so sick?

A wise and incredible friend once told me, "We must not kill any living creature. The killing in itself is bad. We must look out and protect all those who are innocent and vulnerable."

> "Once one accepts the true reality that we – that is, all animals, human and non-human – are all one, the idea of slaughtering animals and eating meat becomes morally unacceptable."[43]
> **Tracey Hamilton**

> "A man can live and be healthy without killing animals for food; therefore, if he eats meat, he participates in taking animal life merely for the sake of his appetite. And to act so is immoral."[44]
> **Leo Tolstoy on Civil Disobedience, Russian Writer**

CHAPTER FIVE
THE OCEANS, OUR LIFELINE

"Seafood is simply a socially acceptable form of bush meat. We condemn Africans for hunting monkeys and mammalian and bird species from the jungle yet the developed world thinks nothing of hauling in magnificent wild creatures like swordfish, tuna, halibut, shark, and salmon for our meals. The fact is that the global slaughter of marine wildlife is simply the largest massacre of wildlife on the planet."[1]
Captain Paul Watson, Founder of *Sea Shepherd Conservation Society*

Fishing: An Environmental Disaster

According to Paul Watson, "we have removed about 90 percent of the fishes from the oceans".[2] Every year, about one to three trillion wild fish and other sea animals are killed.[3] By 2048, it is believed that all our fisheries will be totally wiped out.[4]

Huge ocean liners and drift nets indiscriminately scour the ocean floors, destroying everything in their path, including all the fish.[5] Fish are the oxygen cleaners of our waters, taking in many harmful contaminants and pollutants from the ocean. Without them, life in our oceans would be very different.

By-catch, which refers to catch that is not intended to be caught, is a huge waste of precious life.[6] Various animals such as sea turtles, dolphins, small whales and other animals are also caught indiscriminately when all that the fisherman wanted was one, two or three species at most. A lot of these animals, usually thrown back into the water, are left to slowly die agonizing deaths. The rest of them, who are entangled in the fish nets, slowly die prolonged deaths as well.[7] This is a complete waste of life and food resources. In fact, there are tens of thousands of ships in operation at any one time and devastating ocean ecosystems worldwide.

Do Fish Feel Pain?

Fish are vertebrates with a central nervous system and pain proprioceptors. It is proven that fish definitely do feel and avoid pain. Scientists have found that, when injured, fish and sea invertebrates produce biochemicals such as enkephalins and endorphins that would be excruciatingly painful to humans.[8, 9] The extreme inner weight cracks their swim bladders, pops out their eyes and pushes their stomachs through their mouths. Many of them slowly suffocate or are crushed to death by others that land on them. Others are cut open while still alive.

Many people mistakenly believe fish are cold-blooded animals without any feelings. When fishermen remove them from the water, they flap around convulsively and are slammed against the ground or hit by a rock. This brings about excruciating pain for these animals. We cannot begin to imagine the pain and agony they are going through. If we could hear their screams, we would think twice about fishing or eating them. Since fish do not scream, and only flap around convulsively trying to mitigate the pain, we dismiss their suffering altogether.

> "The scientific literature is quite clear. Anatomically, physiologically and biologically, the pain system in fish is virtually the same as in birds and mammals."[10]
> **Donald Broom, Professor of Animal Welfare at Cambridge University in the UK**

> "I can see no reason whatever to eat fish."[11]
> **Jeffrey Masson, PhD, Bestselling US Author**

One of my favourite passages is that of author Will Tuttle, PhD in his book *The World Peace Diet: Eating for Spiritual Health and Social Harmony*. I think he truly says it all.

"It was drizzling, and I put the first fish I caught into my raincoat pocket, confident he would die before too long. When I caught a second fish, I put her into the other pocket. I went back to the cabin to cook supper, quite proud of myself. The cattail roots and wild carrots were cooking and I went to clean the fish, but to my dismay they were both still alive and flipping about convulsively. I realized that I was killing them, but they were not dead yet, so the old patterns kicked in and I grabbed one and slammed him down hard against the floor. Like waking from a nightmare, I could not believe what I was doing. Yet I did not think I could stop. The fish was still alive! Two more times I had to slam him against the floor, and then the other fish as well, before I could clean them, cook them, and we could eat them for dinner. I could feel their terror and pain, and the violence I was committing against these unfortunate creatures, and I vowed never to fish again. The self-inquiry worked relentlessly to expose my conditioned behaviour and hypocrisy. The old programming that they were "just fish" completely fell away, and I saw with fresh eyes what was actually happening, and how I had entered their world violently and deceitfully with intent to harm. Here I was on a spiritual pilgrimage, trying with all my heart to directly understand the deeper truths of being, yet I was acting contrary to this by first tricking the fish with a lure hiding a cruel barbed hook, and then killing them."[12]

The Largest Massacre on Earth

The Canadian seal slaughter, as recorded by the IFAW (International Fund for Animal Welfare), was the largest slaughter of marine mammals on earth, with a record of 365,971 seals killed in 2004.[13] However, in recent years, this figure has dropped drastically due to the decreasing demand for these products. According to harpseals.org, the numbers went down drastically since 2009. The figures were, at one time, as low as 37,609 seals killed annually.[14]

Most of the seals are babies, killed at three months of age or younger.[15] In most cases, workers use clubs to kill the animals.

On the coast of Taiji, Japan, more than 20,000 dolphins, porpoises, and small whales are beached and killed every year for food and other purposes.[16] Deceiving as it may seem, dolphin meat is sometimes marketed the same as whale meat.[17] It shows how little consideration the Canadian and Japanese governments have for the oceans' ecosystems.

The same is happening to the populations of sharks worldwide. Worldwide, shark populations have declined by some ninety percent. People are even killing whale sharks. Roamers of the seas, these gentle giants only eat krill and have never been reported to have killed a human being. These magnificent creatures are now on the brink of extinction.[18]

We need, not to regulate fishing and whaling industries, but to stop them altogether. No matter how regulated the industry is, fishing is one of the worst destructions to the environment.

CHAPTER SIX
THE WORLD'S RELIGIONS AND SPIRITUAL TRADITIONS

> "You don't need religion to have morals. If you can't determine right from wrong then you lack empathy, not religion."[1]
> **Kane Bailey**

Some of the largest religions in the world are Christianity, Hinduism, and Islam. Other religions or spiritual traditions include Jainism, Judaism and Buddhism.[2] Jainism in India are based on the principle of ahimsa (non-violence or non-injury). Though Hinduism and Buddhism have a large population of vegetarians, Jainism is characterised by its vegetarian principles, the principle of ahimsa (non-violence or non-injury). Vegetarianism (lacto-vegetarianism) is mandatory in Jainism. However, some Jains are vegans.[3]

Over 2000 years ago in ancient Greece, Pythagoras (most likely from what we know of his teachings) taught compassion for all life. His teachings inspired Plato, Plutarch and Plotinus. He and his followers were most likely strict vegetarians (or vegan). People who followed his practices of refraining from eating animals were called Pythagoreans.[4, 5]

> "Forbear, mortals, to pollute your bodies with the flesh of animals. There is corn; there are the apples that bear down the branches by their weight; and there are the grapes, nuts and vegetables. These shall be our food."[6]
> **Pythagoras**

> "As long as men massacre animals, they will kill each other. Indeed, he who sows the seeds

of murder and pain cannot reap the joy of love."[7]

Pythagoras

"The gods created certain kinds of beings to replenish our bodies...they are the trees and the plants and the seeds."[8]

Plato

"Can you really ask what reason Pythagoras had for abstaining from flesh? For my part I rather wonder both by what accident and in what state of soul or mind the first man[…] touched his mouth to gore and brought his lips to the flesh of a dead creature, he who set forth tables of dead, stale bodies and ventured to call food and nourishment the parts that had a little before bellowed and cried, moved and lived. How could his eyes endure the slaughter when throats were slit and hides flayed and limbs torn from limb? How could his nose endure the stench? How was it that the pollution did not turn away his taste, which made contact with the sores of others and sucked juices and serums from mortal wounds?… The obligations of law and equity reach only to mankind, but kindness and benevolence should be extended to the creatures of every species, and these will flow from the breast of a true man, in streams that issue from the living fountain. Man makes use of flesh not out of want and necessity, seeing that he has the liberty to make his choice of herbs and fruits, the plenty of which is inexhaustible; but out of luxury, and being cloyed with necessaries, he seeks after impure and inconvenient diet, purchased by the slaughter of living beasts; by showing himself more cruel than the most savage of wild beasts ... were it only to learn benevolence to human kind, we should be merciful to other creatures ... It is certainly not lions and wolves that we eat out of self-defense; on the contrary, we ignore these and slaughter harmless, tame creatures without stings or teeth to harm us, creatures that, I swear, Nature appears to have produced for the sake of their beauty and grace. But nothing abashed us, not the flower-like tinting of the flesh, not the persuasiveness of the harmonious voice, not the cleanliness of their habits or the unusual intelligence that may be found in the poor wretches. No, for the sake of a little flesh we deprive them of sun, of light, of the duration of life to which they are entitled by birth and being…Why do you belie the earth, as if it were unable to feed and nourish you? Does it not shame you to mingle murder and blood with her beneficent fruits? Other carnivora you call savage and ferocious—lions and tigers and serpents[…] And yet for them murder is the only means of sustenance! Whereas to you it is superfluous luxury and crime!"[9]

Plutarch (c. BCE 46 – CE 120), Greek historian and scholar

In the Islamic, Christian and Jewish religions, we can see many acts of kindness and love, that of veganism. In fact, the act of loving all beings unconditionally is the philosophy of what we today call veganism or vegan living.

"Thou shalt not kill."
(The Ten Commandments, Exodus 20:13 and Deuteronomy 5:17)[10-12]

Nowhere in The Bible does it mention *Thou shalt not kill* only applying to humans. There is no asterisk beside the passage; therefore, it should be taken to mean that we should not kill any living being, human or non-human. People argue, saying that killing plants is also killing life; however in The Bible it does not say that taking the lives of plants is considered killing.

It does say,

> "God said, who told you to kill the bullock and the she goat to make an offering to me? Wash yourself from this innocent blood, so I may hear your prayer; otherwise I will turn my head away because your hands are full of blood. Repent yourself so I may forgive you." (Isaiah 1:11-16)
>
> "But flesh with the life thereof, which is the blood thereof, shall ye not eat." (Genesis 9:4)[13]
>
> "It is good neither to eat flesh, nor to drink wine, nor any thing whereby thy brother stumbleth, or is offended, or is made weak." (Romans 15:21)[14]
>
> And, "God said, I have provided all kinds of grain and all kinds of fruit for you to eat; but for the wild animals and for all the birds I have provided grass and leafy plants for food." (Genesis 1:29)[15]
>
> In The Bible it says, "And God said, Let us make man in our image, after our likeness: and let them have dominion over the fish of the sea, and over the fowl of the air, and over the cattle, and over all the earth, and over every creeping thing that creepeth upon the earth." (Genesis 1:26)[16]

Dominion over animals does not mean that we have the right to exploit or kill them. If you take a closer look at the definition of *dominion* it clearly states, "Rule; authority".[17]

Dominion does not mean to exploit or kill. To have dominion over animals simply means to rule and have authority over them, only to protect and care for them like a parent would do.

It is no surprise that many of the great spiritual leaders of our time may have also been vegetarian or even vegan at some point in their lives. People such as Jesus, Albert Schweitzer, Plotinus, George Bernard Shaw, Mahatma Gandhi, Leonardo Da Vinci, Pythagoras and César Chávez refrained from eating animals.

Some spiritually-minded people such as Mother Teresa, unfortunately, did not make the connection between humans and animals. They were definitely heroes amongst the human population and loved and cared for certain animals, but when it came to farm animals, they were totally oblivious to their suffering.

> "Nowhere in the Bible does it say that we are required to eat animals. Just because the Bible doesn't explicitly forbid something doesn't make it right."[18]
> **Vegan Outreach**

CHAPTER SEVEN
OTHER WAYS WE USE ANIMALS

Animals are also used as pets, in clothing, entertainment, and sports and in animal testing.

Pets

At some point in our lives, we have all likely lived with companion animals. Most of us have a cat or dog and know that when we mistakenly stand on their tail they jump and scream in pain. And when our beloved companion dies, we weep and mourn.

Most of us believe that dogs and cats are obligate carnivores and need meat to survive. Even veterinarians believe this to be so. In nature, cats would be natural carnivores, and dogs omnivores.[1,2] However, cats and dogs are not living in nature, we have domesticated them.

If animals get all the required nutrients in their food then even a vegan diet should be more than sufficient. To my knowledge, cats and dogs can be fed a vegan diet supplemented with certain nutrients like L-carnitine, arachidonic acid, and taurine. However, it is not as simple as giving them vegan food with the needed supplements, careful research is required before doing so.

Today, it is easy for your companion animal(s), dog, cat or ferret to be vegan. With vegan formulas like V-Dog, Ami, and Evolution, transitioning your pet to a vegan diet is healthy and safe.[3-5] With all the required nutrients and added supplements in the formulas, there is no excuse not to feed your pet a more humane alternative to the conventional food on the market.

I have many friends who put their feline friends on Ami Cat and Evolution formula for a while now and they are really healthy according to their veterinarians. Countless people feed their pets vegan food with much success.

Virtually all conventional pet found in stores today contain ingredients from diseased and tortured animals raised on factory farms that are unfit for human consumption. Where do euthanized cats and dogs from pounds and laboratories end up? Some are discarded and thrown in the trash, but a lot of them end up in conventional pet food, turning our companion animals into cannibals.[6] It is no wonder why our pets succumb to the same diseases we have such as certain cancers, intestinal issues, and others illnesses.

Clothing

Fur

Animals who are used for fur are either trapped or live on fur farms. The animals on fur farms endure the same cruel and horrible treatments as the animals used for food endure on factory farms. On fur farms, animals spend their entire lives confined in crowded, filthy, wire cages.[7] These animals are then killed using the cheapest and cruellest methods available including suffocation, vaginal and anal electrocution, gassing and poisoning without any anaesthetics. Some are even thrown against floors or walls, stomped on or have their necks broken.[8]

In China and Korea, millions of dogs and cats are bludgeoned, hung, and bled to death; sometimes they are skinned alive.[9] They are still twitching even after being skinned. There are some two million dogs and cats who are killed annually for their fur, which is then exported to North America.[10, 11]

We do not really know what we are buying because labelling laws in North America are very lax.

Often the fur council will mislabel products specifying the fur as faux (fake) or containing synthetic materials. According to the film Skin Trade by Shannon Keith, faux fur coats, and trimmed jackets were tested to contain animal's skins such as coyotes, mink, rabbit and even cat and dog fur.[12]

Many believe that no one today is buying fur, but the reality is that a lot of people are buying jackets with fur trim, which may look inconspicuous because the manufacturer may dye the trim to match the colour of the jacket. Millions of people around the world continue to buy full-length fur jackets, fur hats and fur gloves, scarves, and boots.

Some people believe manufacturers use scraps of leftovers from animals to make those fur-trimmed jackets. This is not the case as seen in the film *Skin Trade*, the whole animal is used. Sometimes it takes several animals just to make one full-length coat.[13]

Leather

Most leather comes from developed countries like India, where animals regularly have their throats slit and skin ripped off while they are still completely conscious. In India, it is a common practice to slit the throats of cows using blunt knives.[14]

The tanning process requires huge amounts of water, chemicals, metals, dyes, solvents and acids to be used. When we wear fur, leather or other animal skins, we're essentially wearing dead skins and corrosive materials on our bodies. The workers have it even worse. The workers do not wear any shoes or socks and instead, walk barefoot on blood-soaked floors. Workers in tanneries are very often in violation of their health; they wear very little protective clothing such as boots, gloves, and safety glasses. Because of the contact with these potent chemicals, some employees eventually lose their hands, arms, feet or legs.[15]

Down

Down is the soft layer of feathers found closest to a bird's skin. Geese, ducks, and rabbits, either alive or dead, have their feathers or fur violently plucked as they scream in pain and terror. This process is repeatedly done to the same animals, and sometimes rips skin apart and leaves huge wounds that are treated by stitching them in the same unsterile environment in which the animals are plucked. And this is all done without any anaesthetics.[16] Down is then used to make comforters, pillows, parkas, jackets and other wearable products.

Wool

Most of the wool we use comes from Australia. Sheep that are raised for wool have wrinkly skin which produces more wool, but it also attracts more flies and maggots. And because of this, they undergo mulesing, a practice where large chunks of skin and flesh are removed from their backside without painkillers. This process can also attract maggots and flies and cause deadly infections. There is a high demand for wool; therefore sheep are shorn very quickly. This injures the animal and at times, even causes death.[18]

Silk

Silk fabric comes from the silkworm, a moth's larva. There are a few methods for producing silk industrially. Approximately 3000 silkworms are boiled or steamed alive just to produce one pound of silk thread.[19] Just as in industrialized factory farms, silkworms are killed by the millions in cruel and vile ways. There is absolutely no need for silk, just as there is no need for fur, leather, down or wool.

Today there are many synthetic clothing options available in stores, including faux fur, pleather (plastic leather), nylon, polyester, rayon, Tencel, and various silk-type fabrics such as milkweed seed-pod fibres, silk-cotton tree and ceiba tree filaments. Many of these materials such as fake fur, retain the same R-value as animal products.[20] R-value is the measurement of insulation.

> "The time has come for humans and insects to turn towards each other... Such is the way to wisdom, the source of our healing, our guidance into the twenty-first century."[21]
> **Thomas Berry**

Entertainment and Sports

In entertainment and sports, animals are used for bullfighting, horse racing, rodeos, circuses, and zoos. Animals are usually deprived of food and water for a few days before these events.[22] Some animals, such as bulls, are kept in total darkness for days before being released for fighting.[23] Dog-

and cock-fighting are also vindictive and unnecessary. These are considered pleasures for many, but the suffering is relentless. Is it necessary to make a profit from the suffering of animals?

Other hideous ways animals are used are in horse-drawn carriages, aquariums and marine parks, greyhound racing, and various roadside, traveling zoos. These forms of entertainment are unnecessary and cause great pain and suffering to animals. Animals live their whole miserable lives until eventually they die or are killed.

Animal Testing (aka Vivisection)

Every year, millions of rats, mice, rabbits, dogs, cats, primates and other sentient beings suffer and die in cruel ways for pointless scientific and military research. This is called vivisection, where animals are used in experiments or product testing.[24] They endure the same cruel experiments time and time again. Millions are confined to barren cages, fed toothpaste, hand soap, detergents, and toxic chemicals. These chemicals are pumped into their stomachs, rubbed into their skin, dripped into their eyes, and forced into their lungs. They suffer operations without anesthetics; they are burned; and given electric or traumatic shocks.[25-27]

After enduring all this suffering, when they are of no longer of use they are killed and tossed into the trash. Scientists claim this is necessary to prove drugs are safe before they are used on humans, even though, ninety-two percent of drugs that have been shown to be effective and safe on animals, fail on humans and cause adverse side effects and even death.

Who funds these experiments? It is we, the taxpayers. Instead, we should be focusing on disease preventing programs which promote a healthy lifestyle. Human gene studies, human cell cultures, computer models, artificial skin, and test tube studies are commonplace in modern laboratories today.[28] Unfortunately, some of the largest companies in the world such as Procter & Gamble (P&G), Unilever, Church & Dwight, Avon and Nestlé still test on animals even though it has been proven highly ineffective.[29, 30]

"I am not interested to know whether vivisection produces results that are profitable to the human race or doesn't... The pain which it inflicts upon un-consenting animals is the basis of my enmity toward it, and it is to me sufficient justification of the enmity without looking further."[31]

Mark Twain

Today, there are countless alternatives to animal testing which, according to Vegetarian Times magazine, "are not only more ethical, they are also more applicable to human health". Alternatives include selective formulation, human cultures (Epiderm and EpiSkin), skin cultures, surgical specimens, cellular tests, bacteria-based tests, and microdosing.[32]

Not only are these methods more effective and applicable to human health: but also they save more lives, the lives of non-human animals that are routinely beaten, starved and eventually killed and thrown into the trash. Humans' lives are also saved, as they experience better health effects using the products that were tested in a more relevant way.

CHAPTER EIGHT
HUMAN RIGHTS

"Those who consume animals not only harm those animals and endanger themselves, but they also threaten the well-being of other humans who currently or will later inhabit the planet. ... It is time for humans to remove their heads from the sand and recognize the risk to themselves that can arise from their maltreatment of other species."[1]
Michael Greger, MD, Physician, Author and Speaker

Raising animals for food leads to all sorts of human rights issues, such as wars, poverty, famine, social and family issues. All evil stems from oppressing others. When we oppress other living beings, we also oppress other human beings, including ourselves. It cannot be any other way. When we oppress others, it eventually always comes back to us in some way or another.[2]

War

In order to produce animal food, a massive amount of energy is used. Today, more than ever, countries fight over oil. Oil is money and governments and corporations fight for that wealth, power, and land. Why do we need oil? The largest amounts of oil are used for animal agriculture.[3]

When we fund this cruelty which goes on with slaughterhouse and factory farm workers abusing and terrorizing animals, how can we humans be kind and loving to one another? When we cruelly mistreat and slaughter animals, how can we not experience wars among us humans? It cannot be any other way. When wars are happening in the stinking sheds of death called factory farms, the cruelty will mirror itself in humanity, with wars raging amongst us.

> "In fact, our word "capital" derives from *capita*, Latin for "head," as in head of cattle and sheep. The first capitalists were the herders who fought each other for land and capital and created the first kingdoms, complete with slavery, regular warfare, and power concentrated in the hands of a wealthy cattle-owning elite."[4]
> **Will Tuttle, PhD, Author of *The World Peace Diet***

> "Battling others to acquire their cattle and sheep was the primary capital acquisition strategy; the ancient Aryan Sanskrit word for war, *gavyaa*, means literally "the desire for more cattle." It appears that war, herding animals, oppression of the feminine, capitalism, and the desire for more capital/livestock have been linked since their ancient birth in the commodification of large animals."[5]
> **Will Tuttle, PhD, Author of *The World Peace Diet***

Poverty and World Hunger

Because we in the West sell grains at a higher price to give to our livestock, people in third world countries cannot afford to purchase the foods they need to feed their starving children. While they feed themselves, their children starve in their arms. This is why we see the proliferation of poverty and starvation around the world.[6]

According to the World Health Organization (WHO), some 3.7 billion people are malnourished.[7] It is not because we do not have enough food to feed the starving, it is because we feed most of the grains and other plant food to livestock instead of starving people. According to David Pimentel, almost forty percent of grains grown worldwide are fed to livestock.[8] As we in the West overfeed ourselves with animal products, some 40,000 children starve every single day.[9]

It is not hard to understand; the more animal products we consume, the fewer people we can feed. On a meat-based diet we are able to feed roughly two billion people;[10] but on a plant-based diet we are able to feed as many as fifteen billion people.[11] I believe if we cultivated wild plants and grew more fruit trees, we could feed many more people.

Tearing Families Apart

On modern farms today, especially when it comes to the egg, dairy, and veal industries, most babies are stolen from their mothers within a few days of birth and are either killed in one of several inhumane ways [see Chapter Four], or are put into production. Stealing innocent, non-human animal babies from their mothers sows the same in humans, tears families apart, steals and enslaves of children. Again what we do to animals, always boomerangs back to us in countless ways.

Psychological Issues

Psychological issues in humans stem from what we do to animals. Animals in zoos and farms are housed in tiny cages or crates and experience back and forth pacing, mutilation of cage mates and other psychological issues. They go insane from the confinement and suffering. In jails, we can see similar behaviours in humans.

Teen anorexia is on the rise, where mostly teenaged girls starve themselves, become anorexic, just as it is common practice to starve hens to make them lay more eggs (forced moulting).[12] Every known illness and psychological trauma in humans can be traced back to confining, using and killing animals.

Exploited Workers

Slaughterhouse and factory farm workers suffer greatly. In the US, most are forced to take on the job of raising and killing animals to make a living. Most workers are illegal immigrants who, if they report any illegal activities to the authorities, would be threatened with loss of their jobs and deportation back to their home country.[13] This is how the industry protects itself. Every day, workers kill hundreds or even thousands of animals at line speeds so fast that injury and death rates are at an all-time high. Slaughterhouse work is, by far, the most dangerous job in the US today.[14-16]

Turnover rates at these places are 100 percent just after one year of employment.[17] No one wants to do the work. A lot of them do it only temporarily to feed their families. Human beings are not meant to kill living beings like this.

People ask me, "But what about human issues?" I want to ask them in return, what are *they* doing for humans themselves? Slaughterhouse workers, including those who work in factory farms, are probably some of the most abused workers of any industry, physically and psychologically, especially in the US.

If we just consider the fact that everything on our planet is interconnected or interrelated in some way we would understand that most of the problems occurring on the planet today are because of our treatment towards non-human animals. It is no wonder why we have the problems we do today because everything revolves around the exploitation and killing of non-human animals. Do not forget that humans are animals, we are mammals. According to the Oxford Dictionary, an animal is "A living organism which feeds on organic matter, typically having a specialized sense organ and nervous system and able to respond rapidly to stimuli."[18]

> "Until he extends the circle of his compassion to all living things, man will not himself find peace."[24]
>
> **Albert Schweitzer, Theologian, Organist, Philosopher, and Physician**

CHAPTER NINE
CELEBRITIES WHO LIVE THE COMPASSIONATE LIFE

The Ones Who Do not Make the Connection

Like everyone else, there are some celebrities who make the connection and some who do not when it comes to their relationship with other beings.

Unfortunately, there are the celebrities who do not make the connection between their food choices and the beings who suffer from those food choices. Some of these celebrities may have been vegan at one point in their lives then went back to eating animal products. Many of them are probably influenced by industry propaganda or were not fully aware of the issues in the first place. They are the ones who at least somewhat understand the plight of animal suffering and the myriad, interrelated problems that stem from eating them. It is the seed(s) of veganism that are planted in them that raise their consciousness.

Others, like Madonna, the ones who are disputed vegans, are probably not fully aware of the connection between animal food and their negative repercussions.[1] Some of them may consider themselves vegan at certain points in their lives, but hunt, wear fur, or make derogatory remarks about the vegan lifestyle. I believe they too are somewhat confused when it comes to the plight of animal suffering.

The vegan philosophy is about minimizing suffering as much as possible. I wonder why anyone would be vegan one day and go back to consuming animal products the next day. Are they just plain confused? Why is it that vegan celebrities such as Ellen DeGeneres, for example, promote the consumption of eggs, or Alicia Silverstone considers herself vegan while she still consumes dairy on occasion?[2, 3]

I always tell everyone, celebrities are just like the average person; they are no better or worse than the rest of us.

We are all the same. Some of them go back to eating animal food and that is something to consider. They are not bad people, they just were not fully aware of the issue in the first place.

The Ones Who Do Make the Connection

Happily, there are celebrities who do make the connection. There are hundreds if not thousands of celebrities all around the world who are vegan. They include: Moby (singer-songwriter, musician, DJ and photographer), Pamela Anderson (actress and animal rights activist), Joaquin Phoenix (actor, rapper and narrator), Woody Harrelson (actor, activist), Toby Maguire (actor), Martina Navratilova (tennis player), Alanis Morissette (musician), Bryan Adams (musician), Morrissey (musician), Shania Twain (musician), Brendan Brazier (endurance athlete, author and entrepreneur), Sandra Oh (actress), Daryl Hannah (actress), Russel Simmons (entrepreneur), Prince (musician and actor), Carl Lewis (athlete and author), Erykah Badu (musician), Fiona Apple (musician), K.D. Lang (musician), Nelly (rapper), Sinead O'Connor (musician), Avril Lavigne (musician), Bif Naked (musician), and Dennis Kucinich (US politician).[4]

If celebrities can do it, so can the rest of us. It is just cool to be vegan.

Celebrities who do make the change do it for their health, the environment, or both. And some are even becoming more aware that ethics completely includes nonhuman animals. Whatever the reasons, more celebrities are making the connection to a more compassionate diet and lifestyle. A lot of people look up to celebrities and as more of them go vegan, more of us will as well.

CHAPTER TEN
THOSE WHO ARE NOT VEGAN

There are people who claim they are vegan but are not really vegan at all. Even though veganism is different from a mere matter of purity, as vegans we must strive to cause the least harm whenever and wherever possible. I always tell people to do the best they can. If all they can do is buy conventional produce or vegan processed food then do so.

I know a few people who claim to be vegan but have food and other products that are non-vegan, contain animal ingredients or are tested on animals. Products like non-vegan mayonnaise, frozen food, shampoos or hair products and skin creams are found on their shelves. Surely if one claims to be vegan one would check the ingredient list to see if the product is vegan before purchasing it.

Of course, as vegans in a non-vegan world, we may mistakenly purchase non-vegan products. However, if we are negligent and continue to make the same mistakes again and again then that is something to consider more carefully. Some vegans may use non-vegan products just because someone else bought it or they mistakenly purchased it. Maybe there was no vegan alternative at that place and time. Often with enough diligence the appropriate vegan product can be found.

There are some vegans who feed their companion animals non-vegan pet food. These vegans are not fully aware of the implications of doing so. [See Chapter Seven on pets.] If you are a vegan and feed your companion animal(s) conventional pet food, you clearly need to do research on why it is wrong to do so. I would never feed any of my pets (if I had any) such food, just as I would never feed animal food to my children (if I had any). If we claim to be ethical vegans and would not eat these products ourselves, how can we possibly feed them to our companion animals? Isn't that hypocritical on our part?

Even though, I feel as if I am the 'vegan police' when I am with other vegans, to me I wonder if some of these people are really vegan at all. Sometimes it seems that I am just too extreme even for some vegans. There are times when I go to vegan events where they have food items that may contain an animal ingredient. Even though someone probably bought the item by mistake or did not read the ingredient list thoroughly, I believe the product must be removed immediately. However, I have found the opposite with some vegans and vegan events; most people will continue eating or using these products even after knowing they contain an animal ingredient(s).

When I first became vegan in 2009 I still owned non-vegan clothing. Even though I did not purchase any new animal-derived clothing like leather, down or silk, I still wore the old clothes I had. When it came to fur I could not bear wearing the items, so I gave them away. As for leather, I wanted to wear out my leather shoes as I did not have the money to buy new ones. Quality vegan shoes (especially vegan boots) are usually expensive. I went to demonstrations and protests wearing my leather boots and felt like a hypocrite every time I did. I eventually donated all my leather shoes, my wool dress pants, and silk ties.

Vegans who still own animal clothes do so most likely because they cannot afford new ones. Those who can afford new clothes should do so by purchasing vegan garments which may also be second-hand and hopefully fair-trade. Sometimes even friends, family or neighbours may have clothes they do not wear any longer. Ask around. Sometimes websites like Kijiji or Craigslist might have some good deals on quality vegan apparel.[1, 2]

Junk Food Vegans

There are many who are considered 'junk food vegans'. Even long-time vegans still consume highly processed vegan burgers, hot dogs, and other analog meats, vegan cheeses, vegan cakes, cookies, and other types of snacks. These foods are high in fat, salt and processed sugar. Fake meats are good as transitional foods, but are not healthy in the long run.

If we truly want to grow spiritually, we must evolve to eat totally natural food, especially more living food. There is nothing wrong with eating cooked or steamed rice, vegetables and tofu; Asians have eaten this way for thousands of years.[3]

Vibrational frequencies are energy and every living thing is made up of energy.[4] Food is also made up of energy frequencies.[5] That is why, when we consume raw fruits and vegetables, it gives us more energy. Cooked food, especially animal food, leave us feeling bloated and less energized. Hence, when one consumes cooked food, one resorts to lying down and sleeping after the meal.

Different foods vibrate at different frequencies, with processed foods like meat analogues vibrating at low frequencies. Of course animal food, especially those that come from factory farms, are vibrating at the lowest frequencies of all. We want to be eating food with high vibrational frequencies, such as raw, fresh fruit and vegetables, preferably local, eaten fresh right from the earth.

I mention this because anyone who wants more energy and a higher consciousness must include more alkaline food in their diet, especially fruit and vegetables. This is hard to do as we are bombarded with ads for junk food everywhere, especially those promoting animal foods. When one wants to elevate one spiritual level, become enlightened, and calm the mind, one must resort to living closer to nature and resist the distractions of everyday life from the city. As an activist, I often travel to nature to further my spiritual growth. When we quiet our minds, we have better thinking.

As more of us transition from the everyday junk food lifestyle to a more harmonious life, we can expect to find true peace within ourselves. As we reveal the higher part of ourselves, we see the true beauty of the world. And when we see the true beauty of this planet, we experience everlasting joy, love, and happiness. Happiness is not about acquiring material possessions, but about finding inner peace and love and spreading the message to others. Once 'junk food vegans' and others truly find peace within themselves, we will start seeing a more peaceful and beautiful world around us.

Vegan Extremists

We are all on a spiritual path in life. Pythagoras and his disciples, who were open to the ideas of their time, today would still be considered extremists by most. Today, slavery and inequity of non-human animals is also considered normal by most. One day we will look back and laugh at ourselves for considering animal rights to be radical and extreme.

People call vegans extremists. And it is true. We are extremely loving and caring towards all creatures. It is the kindness, love and compassion for all beings that society never accepts. The goodness that stems from our hearts is what is considered *extreme*.

It is true that I and others like me are different. And being different in our society is considered radical and extreme. If we do not eat the same food, dress the same way or talk like everyone else we are considered different. *Extremism* is actually an ideology that stems away from the mainstream or cultural standard.[6] However, when we look at *morality*, we see that it is in our human nature to be kind, loving and compassionate to all beings.[7] This kindness and compassion towards all is the moral baseline of veganism.

As humans, until we go back to our roots of loving-kindness, we will still be savages. Even junk food vegans, until they start implementing a diet of more whole, fresh, raw, living food, cannot reach their highest potential. We need to re-evaluate our lifestyles and do the best that we can to reduce harm. Of course 'junk food vegans,' in my opinion, are still living a more spiritual, loving lifestyle than that of meat eaters, but if we want to reach our highest human potential, we have to elevate our spiritual energy frequencies as high as we can.

> "There's nothing extreme in caring about yourself and caring about animals."[8]
> **Benjamin Zephaniah, Author, poet, and musician**

The Stages of Veganism

In his lectures and interviews, Dr. Will Tuttle talks about the stages of veganism. Though there are three main stages of veganism, there may be more stages beyond this. The first stage is the '*shallow vegan'* stage. One may go vegan for health reasons or because one saw a cruelty video and switched one's diet to include only plant food. Sometimes one eats a lot of vegan junk food and does not fully understand why to go vegan. A lot of people in this stage fall back and eat some meat, dairy, and eggs.

The second stage is called the '*angry vegan'* stage where one understands more of the ideas behind veganism, but one gets angry and judgemental of others. These vegans might shout at people wearing fur or eating animal products and they may view the rest of the world as other and be themselves so viewed. This is not positive vegan advocacy as it deters many away and makes vegans look like extremists.

The polar opposite of angry vegan is referred to as the *'closet vegan'* stage, the polar opposite of the angry vegan stage. A closet vegan is someone, who just wants to keep one's views to oneself and let others do as they please. [See chapter fourteen.]

After this stage comes *'deep veganism'* where one truly understands the vegan message and embodies the lifestyle to the fullest. One lives by example and tries to minimize harm whenever possible and does not get angry or upset when speaking to someone. One sees all animals as sentient beings and does not eat, wear or use any animal products whatsoever. One does not see meat-eaters as different from oneself, but rather as pre-vegans, people who will eventually be vegan in their lifetime. One sees them as one once was oneself, and respects and loves them. One is non-judgemental, non-violent, caring and usually soft-spoken. One addresses people's questions with 'I' statements and not with 'you', as the latter is a form of judgement. After deep veganism, there may be other stages of vegan consciousness. Learning by self-educating, speaking to people and years of experience gives us the knowledge and empowerment to be a better and more efficient vegan activists.

CHAPTER ELEVEN
DO PLANTS FEEL PAIN?

According to science, plants do not have a brain or central nervous system; therefore they cannot experience pain. They can, however, respond to stimuli, which is very different from pain.

While I believe all things on this planet have a life force, we must remember that mobile beings such as humans and animals are the only ones that experience feelings such as pain, happiness and other sensations. There is still no scientific evidence that plants experience the same kinds of sensations.[1] Even if plants could feel pain, it still does not give us the right to continue torturing and killing animals as we please.

Further, we know, just by looking at plants, that they are not mobile, they do not scream and they do not run away. Though some may argue that fish do not scream either, they do move about and gasp convulsively when taken out of the water. We know that when fish flap around they are experiencing discomfort and pain.

When we look at nature, we ask ourselves this question: has Mother Earth endowed plants to feel, or did she create them for animals to consume? Did she create rocks, sand and the soil beneath our feet to feel something? Even though I believe everything on this planet has some sort of energy life force, cutting into plants like cabbage or bananas is very different from cutting into sentient beings like cows, pigs or fish. We know it takes more water, energy, land, and plants when we consume animal food compared to a vegan diet. In the end, more plants are consumed when we eat a meat-based diet.

As humans, we have to understand the true meaning of life, which is simply to minimize harm and suffering and take care of the planet and one another.

Plants certainly, in my opinion, are alive. I am not sure if they actually feel pain or not, but they are definitely alive.

But even if one still believes plants feel pain, perhaps it is alright for us to eat fruits, as the tree does not suffer or die for us to eat the fruits.

> "There's a thing about growing plants (that was typically women's work) and brings out the best in us in a sense of working with nature and with the cycles of life and with the abundance and creativity of life."[2]
>
> **Will Tuttle, PhD, Author of *The World Peace Diet***

> "For plants to feel physical pain, they must have some sort of organized tissue which, upon stimulation, would activate a structure in the plant that is conscious and could perceive the stimulation as painful. There are no structures within plants that are analog to the pain receptors, neurons, and pain-perceiving portions of the brains of vertebrate animals. Animals, being mobile, benefit from their ability to sense pain; but plants simply have no biological or evolutionary need for the experience of pain. Even if, contrary to all evidence, plants did feel pain, it would still be preferable to be vegan. More plants are killed in non-vegan diets, as more plants must be harvested to feed animals."[3]
>
> **Vegan Outreach**

CHAPTER TWELVE
LOVE IS THE ANSWER

> "If we don't love ourselves, we would not love others. When someone tell[s] you to love others first, and to love others more than ourselves; it is impossible. If you can't love yourselves, you can't love anybody else. Therefore we must gather up our great power so that we know in what ways we are good, what special abilities we have, what wisdom, what kind of talent we have, and how big our love is. When we can recognize our virtues, we can learn how to love others."[1]
> **Supreme Master Ching Hai, poet, painter, musician, writer, and entrepreneur**

Why We Must Love Everyone

Howard Lyman, fourth-generation cattle rancher, and author of the book *Mad Cowboy*, said in the documentary *Peaceable Kingdom: The Journey Home*,

> "We are here in my opinion as *Homo sapiens* on this planet to learn one thing. And that one thing is unconditional love. Not unconditional love just for humans, not unconditional love just for the environment, but unconditional love for our entire community on this planet."[2]

Howard Lyman is absolutely right, *unconditional love* is the answer. Unconditional love includes all beings, not just humans, but all. In the film *Vegucated*, he goes on to say,

> "I just revel in the fact that I am able to come here and spend time with people who have the

> opportunity to change the world. And from the bottom of my heart, I will tell you that we need to change the world, or our society as we know it will not survive."[3]

I believe the only way we will ever survive is by loving all creatures, big and small. When we love, the love radiates back to us in countless ways. We may not realize the immediate effects, but we will feel more joy and happiness when we love more and more.

Love is the only way. To love is the most benevolent thing one can do, even for slaughterhouse and farm workers. Yes, they also need our love. Even though some of us may feel hate or anger towards them, we must understand that they were born in a culture like the rest of us, forced to consume animal food, and it is nothing of their own doing. We have to also remember that most of them take on these jobs out of desperation or the lack of work, just to earn a living. Why be angry or hateful towards them? We must instead see love in everyone and everything. Bad karma just leads to more bad karma.[4, 5] The basic philosophy of veganism is to love all beings. If we do not love everyone, including meat-eaters (or pre-vegans) and the ones who do the slaughtering, how can we be considered compassionate and loving vegans? As we see love in everyone, we radiate more love into our lives and into the world around us.

Although I have seen some of the most terrible abuse towards animals carried out at a slaughterhouse, the workers are not the ones to blame. If I were to go there and try to stop the atrocities from happening what good would it do? The industry will continue its abusive practices. What we need to do is love the slaughterhouse workers and believe that, one day, they will awaken, as will the industry and the consumers. Do not forget that we (the consumers) are the ones who demand the products. The industry is supplying the demand. On the outside, it may seem that the slaughterhouse workers are at fault, but truly, no one only is at fault. Universally, as *Homo sapiens,* we must evolve to a higher consciousness, a new spirituality. How did we ever grow spiritually in the opposite direction to become violent people, destroying and killing everything on the planet? No one really knows, but if we continue to love and care for one another, magical things can happen.

As humans, violence hurts us. Even though we may feel the need to lash out with hateful remarks or even cause violence towards those who cause abuse, this is not the solution. We must unconditionally love everyone, including those who are abusive to others.

Harold Brown is a former animal farmer who is featured in the film *Peaceable Kingdom: The Journey Home*,

> "People asked me, well, how on Earth could you have ever done that? And, it is a very hard question to answer. How do you do it? How do you, you know, kill the animal, how do you find it within yourself to kill and butcher it? As time went by, you just realized you needed to keep a certain amount of distance emotionally from the animals, so you trained yourself. It was a discipline like anything else."[6]

Ever sincc we were little children, the love and compassion that was innate in us has been hidden and suppressed. In every one of us lies a truly loving and caring person. In order to awaken our true, innate wisdom, one must experience a deep revelation from within.

Mahatma Gandhi was right in telling his followers, even when physically abused by others, to show love and mercy to those abusers and to never use violence. Even Martin Luther King, Jr. understood this when he delivered his sermon at the Dexter Avenue Baptist Church in Montgomery, Alabama, on Christmas Day, 1957:

> "First, we must develop and maintain the capacity to forgive. He who is devoid of the power to forgive is devoid of the power to love. It is impossible even to begin the act of loving one's enemies without the prior acceptance of

> the necessity, over and over again, of forgiving those who inflict evil and injury upon us. It is also necessary to realize that the forgiving act must always be initiated by the person who has been wronged, the victim of some great hurt, the recipient of some tortuous injustice, the absorber of some terrible act of oppression."[7]

In the book *Peace to all Beings* by Judy Carman, there is a story that sums this up beautifully.

> "A thief entered the cottage of Pavahari Baba to steal what he could. When Pavahari Baba returned home and saw the thief, he ran after him offering more, pleading with him to come back and get all that he needed. In awe of the response, the thief never stole again and became a disciple of Pavahari."[8]

We can view this story as a lesson in forgiving those who do bad deeds. It is hard to understand what is going on in their minds unless we are they. Their stories are unique; we must not judge anyone.

As a young child, just like everyone in our culture, I ate large quantities of meat, dairy, and eggs. I was not an evil person; I was taught from a young age by my parents and all institutions that this was the way we were supposed to eat. I did not question it.

Over the years, I began seeing and feeling myself in others. We are interconnected. This is what love is, we have to have empathy for others. When we care for one another and love unconditionally, we live our true purpose. As animals, human and non-human, we want to live our purpose without pain and suffering. However, to fulfill our true human potential we need to alleviate as much suffering as possible. This means that we must love all animals as well as one another.

If we were walking down the street and saw someone beating a dog, wouldn't we want to do something to stop it? If we saw someone beating a pig or chicken wouldn't we want to do something to stop it? Any rational human being would most likely try to stop any form of cruelty that one sees, but do we ever stop to think of the endless violence our food causes to animals in farms and slaughterhouses? No! If we say we are opposed to cruelty towards animals then it is time we start caring about all animals, including the ones we think of as food. It should go without saying that we should treat our companion animals, such as dogs and cats, with love and compassion, and give the same love to pigs, chickens, turkeys, cows and other farmed animals. To love and care for only certain types of animals is incredibly hypocritical and inconsistent with our view of animals. If we are eating hamburgers, hot dogs, pepperoni pizzas or fillets of fish, do we really care about animals?

On the outside, it may seem as if we do not care about farm animals, but deep in our hearts, we really do care. If we are given the chance to experience a scenario like the one above, we would try to stop the violence because we know violence of any sort is wrong and we must stop it. Why don't we see and understand the immense violence behind the steak, hamburger, milk and eggs we consume? Why is it that only when we witness cruelty right in front of us, do we act upon it? Why is it that some of us who witness cruelty footage rationalize their diet choices as if they do not cause harm?

It is a *food prison* that we are part of. As Albert Einstein said,

> "A human being is a part of the whole, called by us the "Universe," a part limited in time and space. He experiences himself, his thoughts and feelings, as something separated from the rest—a kind of optical delusion of his consciousness. This delusion is a kind of prison for us, restricting us to our personal desires and to affection for a few persons nearest to us. Our task must be to free ourselves from this Metaphysics of Food prison by widening our circle of compassion to embrace all living

creatures and the whole of nature in its beauty."[9]

There are also some who could not care less about animals. Although I believe all humans are compassionate by nature, these people simply do not care about lives of others. I believe these people are deeply entrenched in cultural programming and are so blind that nothing matters except their own selfishness. These people also need our love.

Everything and everyone is interconnected in some way. Life evolves from the earth where nutrients are given back to the plants and we get nourishment directly from those plants. Pandas, tigers, lions, elephants, zebras, alligators, sharks, whales and dolphins and dogs, cats, fish, rabbits, chickens, pigs, cows, ducks and horses are all here for some purpose. They are on this planet for a reason. All animals feed nutrients to the earth through their bodies and bodily fluids. They all have a purpose that they want to fulfill. Just like us; they can breathe, procreate, feel pain and experience happiness.

We tend to disregard animals and their amazing characteristics and abilities; fishes' ability to live in water, birds' ability to fly, insects' and other animals' abilities to burrow, live in and out of water or adapt to extreme temperatures. We carry none of these traits, but we consider ourselves superior to these beings. Is it because of our technology or language that we consider ourselves superior to them? Or is it because we can dominate and abuse them? And even though we can swim, fly and survive in extreme cold or hot situations, we cannot do it so well as other animals can and not at all without modern technology.

In nature, animals kill only if it is necessary for their survival, but humans have no reason to kill for food or any other purpose. Even the Inuit in arctic regions now have access to food from the south just as they have to modern transpiration, communication and other technology. Unfortunately their heavy meat/fish laden diet has lead to short lifespans and very high rates of osteoporosis as well. Humans are tropical beings; we are not meant to live in the Arctic anyway.[10, 11] In our modern world, there is access to supermarkets, so we can easily be vegan.

> "Kindness and compassion towards all living beings is a mark of a civilized society. Only when we have become non-violent towards all life will we have learned to live well ourselves."[12]
> **César Chávez, Farm Worker, Labour Leader and Civil Rights Activist**

Veganism Is Love

It is good to understand the history behind the word *vegan*. The term vegetarian was documented to be used as early as 1842 (some say even as early as 1838 and 1839), but was only popularized after the formation of the Vegetarian Society in 1847.[13] In 1944, in England, Donald Watson coined the term *vegan* (pronounced vee-gn) and founded The Vegan Society. Donald Watson wanted a better definition that included all sentient beings in the circle of compassion.

> "Veganism denotes a philosophy and way of living which seeks to exclude—as far as is possible and practical—all forms of exploitation of, and cruelty to, animals for food, clothing, or any other purpose; and by extension, promotes the development and use of animal-free alternatives for the benefit of humans, animals, and the environment."[14, 15]

Watson created the word based on kindness and compassion for animals and not for health or environmental concerns (even though veganism does benefit our health and help the environment). While vegetarians refrain from consuming flesh (including seafood); they may, however, consume dairy and/or eggs, may wear animal clothing and/or use other animal products and/or support animal industries like circuses or marine parks. These people are called lacto-ovo vegetarians; lacto means dairy, and ovo means eggs.[16] A vegetarian diet was originally referred to as a vegetable diet, without animal products, but today people who eat eggs, dairy and even fish and chicken consider themselves vegetarian. Therefore, according to the original meaning, no one can consider themselves vegetarian because it is not possible to consume only vegetables, as we would be deficient in many nutrients and possibly get sick in the long term. That's why I like using the word vegan because it includes all beings in the sphere of our compassion.

Honey, however, is one of those foods that is disputed within the vegan community. Are you vegan if you consume honey? Simply put, honey is an animal product; it is regurgitated food that comes from the stomachs of bees, therefore it cannot be considered vegan.[17]

If we believe in peace and unconditional love, we must include all beings in our sphere of concern. Peace means just that, to acknowledge that we are all one, that we are all interconnected, each with our own purposes, drives, and feelings. As animals, we are all living and breathing creatures. As A. C. Bhaktivedanta Swami Prabhupada said,

> "The animal is eating, you are eating; the animal is sleeping, you are sleeping; the animal is defending, you are defending; the animal is having sex, you are having sex; the animals have children, you have children; you have a living place, they have a living place. If the animal's body is cut, there is blood; if your body is cut, there is blood. All the similarities are there. In logic this is something called analogy. Analogy means drawing a conclusion by finding many points of similarity. If there are so many points of similarity between human beings and animals, why deny one similarity? That is not logic. That is not science."[18]

All animals, even the common housefly, and earwig, have their place in this world; they have their own purpose. The common housefly pollinates flowers and fruit trees and they are food for birds and many other animals. Tiny animals and microorganisms also have a purpose to fulfill in the soils, trees and other ecosystems in the environment. Birds take care of mosquitoes and other insects, and insects take care of smaller microbes and other tiny organisms in the soil.

Top carnivorous species such as wolves, sharks, and lions have their fundamental purpose in the universe as well.

Even then, I really do believe in Mango Wodzak's vision of a day when even tigers and lions will sit compassionately beside the gazelles and zebras in peace. This is depicted in The Bible, with Adam and Eve in the Garden of Eden. Everything was peaceful and all animals were at peace with one another. I believe a world like this is possible if we practice and envision it.

> "We need, in a special way, to work twice as hard to help people understand that the animals are fellow creatures, that we must protect them and love them as we love ourselves."[19]
> **César Chávez, Farm Worker, Labour Leader and Civil Rights Activist**

> "Until one has loved an animal, a part of one's soul remains unawakened."[20]
> **Anatole France**

> "The love for all living creatures is the most noble attribute of man."[21]
> **Charles Darwin**

CHAPTER THIRTEEN
MAKING THE TRANSITION

Human Consciousness

In order to raise our consciousness, we must be fully awakened. Our thoughts need to be focused on saving ourselves from our own disasters. Adopting a vegan lifestyle is the first step when making this transition. Meditation is also important in transforming ourselves and the world around us. As more of us become aware of the positive effects of veganism, we will start experiencing those same positive energies all around us.

Looking back, we will see how disastrous we were, forcing violence and cruelty upon each other and upon the earth. In the future, with our intelligence and technology, we can only hope for a better world of peace and harmony. When I look back at how things were before, I cannot believe we have come this far. But there is still more work to be done.

The earth is about 4.5 billion years old.[1, 2] We have lived here for just a short fraction of this time. Every one of us is a link to the future; every seed planted is a hope for human progress. It is time that we seriously look at the issues and we can start by looking at what's on our plates.

What we do from here on in, how we mentally and spiritually connect with the world, is up to each and every one of us. As rational human beings, we can either adopt a vegan lifestyle, choosing to live in the Garden of Eden or we can continue destroying this beautiful, loving home we call planet Earth.

> "As long as we remain, at core, a culture that sees animals merely as commodities and food, there is little help for our survival."[3]
> **Will Tuttle, PhD, Author of *The World Peace Diet***

Transitional Food

It is even easier to become a vegan in today's modern world. As you read in Chapter Three, The Vegan Food Guide, there are many analog transitional food on the market today, which are designed to make the change to veganism even easier. Unlike thirty or even twenty years ago, when there were a few bland and tasteless meat alternatives on the market, today there are in stores many meat alternatives that taste very much like the original animal products. Most of these alternatives are found in supermarkets from coast to coast. Some products are not that great while others are pretty tasty. Some are made from soy, others from wheat gluten or rice. Be aware, not all meat, milk or cheese alternatives are vegan, some may be vegetarian. Usually, meat alternatives will have the vegan symbol on the back. If you are unsure, check the ingredients or call the company to make sure that the product is 100% vegan.

There are vegan deli slices, fake turkeys, veggie dogs and burgers, vegan pizza, ribs, bacon, fish, chicken and more. Some food, like imitation crab, for example, are not even vegetarian; they are made from fish. So do not be tricked by the words imitation or fake and conclude that it is a vegan product. Make sure it has an ingredient list.

Most fake meats have more than one ingredient, usually with soy, rice or gluten as the base. Milk alternatives including soy, almond, rice, and also hemp, coconut, oat, spelt, rye, quinoa, flax, sunflower, hazelnut, and cashew are now more delicious and affordable than ever. Virtually all local stores now carry some brand of soy, rice or almond milk. Some non-dairy beverages are fortified with added vitamins and minerals like B_{12}, calcium, and vitamin D, and some are organic. Often you can find plant-based milks in a variety of flavours such as plain, original, vanilla and chocolate [buy only if it says fair trade chocolate/cocoa], or even fruit flavoured like mango and strawberry. There are now even soy and coconut coffee creamers. Please be aware that not all non-dairy milks are vegan. Check the ingredients or contact the company to be sure. Some may add natural flavours that may be animal-derived or they may be fortified with lanolin-based vitamin D_3.

Vegan cheeses are also to be found. They are made from soy, rice or cashews. Be wary however as some soy cheeses may contain a milk protein called casein (sometimes called caseinate or sodium caseinate). Vegan cheeses come in blocks, grated form, or slices. Some melt while others do not. Each has its own unique flavour and taste. There are also many specialty cheeses on the market. Vegan parmesan cheese, cream cheese, and ricotta are just a few. These cheeses can be found in health food stores or larger supermarkets.

There are many brands and flavours of vegan ice creams, yogurt and other dairy alternatives available as well. Some are organic while others are not. Essentially any dairy product today now exists in vegan form.

It is also easy to replace eggs, milk and honey in baking and cooking. While it may take some time to experiment and find what works best for different applications, you may find vegan alternatives actually cheaper, in the long run, compared to animal products.

For more information on vegan alternatives to animal products visit http://thevegansandwich.com/vegan-alternatives

> "For the first twenty-seven years of my life, I ate animals and animal secretions. However, during my time at Farm Sanctuary, I didn't think about how I used to harm animals. I just enjoyed myself. I petted the animals. I looked into their eyes. I felt love for them. I felt grateful that they were in a place where they could be themselves. They could interact with nature. They could interact with each other."
> **John Sakars, Animal Rights Activist**

Cost

If you take a basic vegan lifestyle, calculate the cost, and compare it to a meat diet, you will clearly see that the vegan diet is overall less expensive. If you buy essential foods like vegetables, fruits, whole-grains, nuts, seeds and legumes and supplement your diet with B_{12}, it is overall less expensive compared to the Standard American Diet (SAD).[4] An omnivorous type diet not only includes meat, dairy, eggs, fruits and vegetables, it also includes costs for pharmaceutical medications and hospital visits that are associated with the diet.

It may seem that in the short-term, eating fast food is inexpensive; who cannot afford a ninety-nine cent burger? But in the long-term, both for the pockets and health of many, it may actually not be the cheapest option.

People who are eating at fast-food places are sick, unhealthy and have to endure medical costs associated with their lifestyle. Even those who are eating home cooked meals full of animal products are sick and deprived of vital energy [see Chapter Three, Health Implications]. It is no wonder why millions of people today are hospitalized with serious health conditions. A few times a year sickness runs through the family; someone is infected with the cold or flu virus. It is inevitable that those who consume animal products will be, some time or another, sick and visiting the doctor or hospital. This means they will have to pay medical costs and take time off work, school and/or family life.

Time is money and time away from work, school or any other function is incvitable when one has a meat-eating addiction. In the long-term, if we want to save money and put it to good use for environmental preservation or other causes, veganism is the ideal lifestyle to choose.

However, there may be times when veganism can be quite costly. If one is buying processed foods such as meat alternatives (like veggie burgers or soy cheeses) or buying all organic, it can get quite costly compared to the Standard American Diet. I should point out that these transitional foods are only for the first stages of veganism when letting go of animal products is difficult. Later on, it is better to move on to whole-plant foods. Today, veganism is easier than ever and no one has to suffer and die for our meals.

When we understand the true costs associated with a meat-centred diet, the costs of imprisoning animals, destroying the environment and in turn, making ourselves sick, we can see why, in the end, veganism is the best way to live.

CHAPTER FOURTEEN
WHY WE MUST PROMOTE COMPASSION

Why Become an Activist?

As we transition to the vegan lifestyle it is not only important for us to strive to do the best we can when making purchases, but to also spread the compassionate message to others. Once we understand the objections to raising animals for food [see Chapters Four and Five], and view videos such as Farm to Fridge and 10 Billion Lives, we will want to start spreading the vegan message to as many people as possible.[1, 2] How can one not want to spread the message to the world after witnessing such unthinkable cruelty?

As we know, a vegan saves some thousands of animals in one's lifetime, but as activists and educators, we each can save thousands more. If we are quiet and shy, keeping our views to ourselves, how do we expect things to get any better on this planet? We know millions upon millions of animals are being brutally tortured and slaughtered for human consumption. It is our duty to be a voice for them.

After looking into the eyes of the terrified farm animal, it is our obligation to save them and be their guardians. If we believe it is our own personal choice to not consume animal products and think we should not push our beliefs on others, we are forgetting about animals themselves. They do not have a choice; they are being brutally murdered every single day because of greed. We have an obligation to do whatever we can to help them. We must, of course, do this in the most loving and caring way possible. We can do this, not by arguing with people, but by telling our story of how we became vegan, and being an example. I think this is one of the best ways of promoting veganism.

I believe it is also a good idea to spread the vegan message as far and wide as we can. I leave vegan pamphlets in buses, streetcars and subways, libraries and other high traffic areas. Order materials from grassroots organizations or create our own. Advertise the vegan message by wearing vegan t-shirts and other vegan apparel as often as I can.

There are millions who suffer because of our meat-eating society. It is not enough to change our food and lifestyles, we must also be a voice for animals. Presently, there is much more destruction than people going vegan. As much as we spread the vegan message, in our so doing many find that animals have done even more for us then we on their behalf.

Undoubtedly, it is the greatest thing we can do not only for animals, but also for our own sanity. We are here for one another, not nearly for our own selfish endeavours. Understanding interconnectedness with all life and the urgency of the matter propels us to do more. It is not enough that we become vegan; we need to get out there and talk to as many people as we can.

I always tell people, even if I talk to just one person, a seed is planted which could potentially sprout into something larger. If that person starts spreading the vegan message and gets others to do the same and so on, there will be a domino effect, which will affect many people and raise the consciousness on the planet.

Once we realize the urgency of the situation we will understand our true purpose and the meaning of life. When we realize our true purpose, nothing else is of concern. No more will we care about jobs, houses, money, prestige, or materialistic lifestyles. Of course, there will be times when one will need money or material possessions to survive and teach others the message of unconditional love and caring for all beings.

I found it was time to start looking squarely at the issue. The time had come for me to decide if I would follow the crowd or take the issue into my own hands. No one could help me; it is up to me to decide what to do from here on to help the planet. I had to ask myself; "How important is animal ethics? Did I want to spread the message of compassion?" So the path I have chosen now is my passion and purpose in life.

CHAPTER FIFTEEN
HOW MEAT KILLS US AND VEGANISM SAVES THE WORLD

The Implications of Meat-Based Diets – Summery of Why It is Wrong to Eat Animals

As aforesaid, humans' flesh-eating habits are destroying the planet; meat is making us sick and killing billions of innocent animals. There are hundreds of billions if not trillions of animals, from both land and sea that are slaughtered every year for our food consumption. Even if we were to breed and slaughter more animals we would not be able to feed the entire world or sustain our planet. Even if we consumed grass-fed, free roaming animals, the process would not be sustainable.[1]

Although various estimates exist as to how many people are overweight and obese, World Watch Institute considers it is around two billion, and that on the other hand, the malnourished number 3.7 billion.[2, 3] From this, we can see that we need a new paradigm shift if we are ever to survive on this planet. We need to change our lifestyle and eating habits to include more fruit and vegetables in our diet and fewer processed and refined foods. Fat intake needs to be minimized and animal products eliminated.

We would not be eating the vast quantities of animals we do today if we were limited to small family farms. It would not be possible to sustain our meat-eating lifestyles with family farming. According to the Food and Agriculture Organization of the United Nations, worldwide per person, annual meat consumption in 2009 was up to 41.9 kilograms. The World Health Organization estimates meat consumption in the mid-1960s was around 24 kilograms. In the late 90's, that number went up to about 36 kilograms. In 2010, that number was almost 42 kilograms. While in the developing world the consumption is about 32 kilograms, in the industrialized world it is up to 80 kilograms.[4, 5]

Our meat-eating addiction and desire to stuff our faces with fast food is leading to tens of thousands of children starving at this very moment. I see the world much differently from how I did many years ago. Not only do I witness a lot of suffering, but I also feel the suffering and sadness in my heart.

We feed most of the harvested grains, legumes and soybeans to farmed animals. This is one of the main causes of world hunger. We could be feeding the food to humans instead, and not breeding animals for meat and other products.[6]

Scientists estimate that every day, 150 to 200 animal and plant species become extinct; we are left to wonder what would happen if animals higher on the food chain were to go extinct.[7] Forests and oceans are the lungs of the earth; they take in carbon dioxide and release oxygen.[8] Without them, there most likely would not be life on Earth. Therefore, we need to be careful about what we do to the environment. Topsoil loss, droughts, climate change, and deforestation are also important issues that need to be taken into consideration.

Animal products are not only destroying the environment and causing harm to animals, they are also making us very sick. Every year, millions upon millions of people end up in hospital beds due to some sort of illness. We did not inherit the flu or the common cold, cancer, heart disease or diabetes, something has gotten us there. Plants do not cause these illnesses and they are not genetically inherited or caused by our environment. Most of the ailments and diseases are caused by our meat-eating addictions.[9]

> "The reason meaty diets have a strong hold on people is because they trigger the release of opiates in the brain. The opiates tend to act as feel-good drugs, just as any other narcotic drug would."[10]
>
> **Neal Barnard, MD**

Energy consumption, water, land use, and desertification are other serious issues we are faced with. As mentioned before, the main cause of these and other serious environmental issues is the rearing of animals for food. We are killing the planet.

As discussed in Chapter Four, Animal Agriculture, animals (especially on factory farms) face gruelling and tortured lives. Pigs, chickens, turkeys, cows and other animals face brutal mutilations and beatings, and if dogs and cats were so treated, people could be faced with cruelty charges.

Similar things are happening in the oceans and their creatures. Huge ships are scouring the ocean floors, tearing up everything in their path. Nothing is left, they go about wrecking precious coral reefs and catching millions upon millions of sea life, what the industry calls bycatch.[11] According to Captain Paul Watson, founder of the Sea Shepherd Conservation Society, "We have removed about ninety percent of the fishes from the oceans."[12] This has serious implications not only for ocean life, but on our own survival as well. If we were to kill the majority of life on the planet, we probably would not be alive. Fish take in many harmful contaminants and, without them, our oceans would be toxic sludge.[13]

We have known for some time now that non-human animals feel pain just as we do, and of course feel it when killed.[14] Still we slaughter them by the billions. Factory farms and slaughterhouses are sheer terror for our fellow brothers and sisters. And no matter how animals are raised, free range, free roaming, cage-free, antibiotic-free, organic, Halal, Kosher, or so-called humane, all these animals end up killed.[15] And when the slaughter lines are running at ever-higher speeds, the cruelty only increases.

As noted in Chapter Four, Animal Agriculture, no slaughter is truly humane. And if you still believe there must be some way to humanely slaughter and raise animals, you are fooling yourself. Just ask yourself, if you were in the animal's position, would you want to be raised and slaughtered long before your time, just so someone can eat you? In our evolutionary biology how did we become so violent, and how can we repair the damage we have caused?

The Vegan Imperative – How Veganism Can Save the World

We can never expect to find peace, unity or love amongst ourselves if we continue consuming animal products. Only when we all adopt the vegan way of living will there ever be peace, love and harmony amongst us.

Food will be diverted from monocultures that feed farmed animals to veganic (organic without any animal inputs such as manure or blood meal) orchards that will feed us all. Livestock will no longer graze in the Amazonian rainforests, thriving wildlife and forests as abundant as they once were. Oceans and coral reefs will be teaming with life so plentiful that there will be a balance in the ecosystem. Hospitals will be a thing of the past. No longer will there be a need for pharmaceutical medications as heart disease, cancer, diabetes and many other illnesses will be eliminated.

Being kind is innate in us. We are born kind and loving, with no worries in the world. As young children, we are taught by a culture that sees animals merely as property. It is nothing we have ever undertaken on our own. As we get older, it seems normal, natural and necessary to eat animal food. We do not question it because we have been told by our parents and relatives, school systems, religious institutions, doctors and the medical profession, advertising and media, corporations and governments that it is normal to be consuming these types of foods. Everyone is doing it, so why shouldn't we? Killing innocent beings, however, is not normal, and by being vegan we pledge to be their voice. They cannot speak our language, and they are totally defenceless, and at our mercy; therefore we need to be their guardians.

Non-human animals almost never retaliate against us. I believe this is because they forgive us for what we do to them. They love us and pray for us, even though we do not know precisely what they are thinking when they are being trucked off to the slaughterhouses. I do believe that animals know their life is coming to an end. They scream and bellow when they enter the slaughterhouse, they see their brothers and sisters in front of them going to their deaths. They are not stupid; they know death is approaching them.

As animals continue loving and praying for us, it means that we should do the same for them. Being vegan is the ultimate protest against their enslavement and abuse. Once we feel compassion for all life we will start awakening to the true beauty of this planet. Everyone will have an abundance of fresh, clean food, water and a place to live.

Humans will start making a decent living; there will be no more child and slave workers. Corporations and governments will want to help us, will put subsidies into growing food, rather than killing for food. When we work in harmony with the earth and one another, we bring out the best of ourselves.

We can have all this if we really want. The Garden of Eden is within us all; we can have orchards and everyone can live in harmony. Let us rejoice all our brothers and sisters, both in the non-human and human world, along with Mother Earth who supplies her divine, nourishing love to all of us. Once we accept that we are all interconnected, we will then find peace.

CHAPTER SIXTEEN
FRUITARIANISM: THE GARDEN OF EDEN

What is Fruitarianism?

The definition of fruitarianism has been somewhat diluted over the years to mean pretty much anything. Like veganism, which is not just a diet, fruitarianism is an ethical and spiritual lifestyle. If one truly wants to grow spiritually, one must look at a fruitarian way of living.

When we take the word fruitarian and break it down, we come up with fruit and arian. To me, it is a diet and lifestyle where all the calories come from the flesh around the seed of the fruit. Even though I try to get most of my calories from fruits, sometimes it is not possible due to location, cost or other factors. As I always say, "do the best you can".

Because the word fruitarian has been misused over the years, Mango Wadzak coined the term "Eden Fruitarianism [which] involves eating or genuinely aspiring to eat a diet consisting of 100 percent raw fresh fruit".[1] It is much more than a diet though. It is a lifestyle that was once practised by Adam and Eve in the Garden of Eden.

Why Fruitarianism?

As outlined in Mango Wodzak's book *Destination Eden*, there is now a new way of reaching the Garden of Eden. In order to propose such a world, we need to live the way Adam and Eve once did, with fruit as the centre of our lifestyle. It is the least harmful way of living. However, there will be times when perfect harmony cannot exist. We may step on insects or plant fruit trees that harm or kill small animals in the process, but we can strive to cause the least harm possible.

Fruit, by far, if grown veganically and locally or wild, is a more sustainable and loving way to live compared to any other food. Fruit even imported from afar and grown conventionally is healthier and more sustainable than all forms of animal or even plant agriculture. It causes the least harm to the planet and to every living creature. If we practise this lifestyle with love, replicating the way we used to live in nature, in time we will be living in the Garden of Eden. The Garden of Eden is a place where no harm occurs. It is a place of tranquility and love, with everyone living in harmony with one another. Of course, it may take hundreds or even thousands of years to reach the Garden of Eden, but nonetheless, striving for such a place is possible. If harm were caused in the Garden of Eden, it would be unavoidable harm. All the avoidable forms of harm, such as fishing, animal farming, and deforestation, would cease to exist. Nature would bountifully offer fruit as our main fuel source. Cars and other modes of transportation would be fuelled with carbohydrates from fruits[2], vegetable oils, water and/or solar power from the sun.

As we compare different types of foods, we can say that animal products, as we have learned, cause tremendous suffering for everyone. It can also be said that the growing of grains is almost as bad for the environment as animal products. Grains, by far, out of all plant food, are the most destructive food source on the planet. Not only does it take more energy, water, and land to produce grains compared to fruits, growing fields of grain destroys the homes of millions of animals, driving many to the brink of extinction.

According to the book *Grain Damage* by Dr. Douglas Graham, "An acre of fruit trees will feed 250% more people than an acre of grain." He also said, "In terms of yield in pounds per acre, grains are the least productive of all plant foods".[3]

> "Grains[…] due to their environmentally destructive mono-crop natures, and need for heavy post-harvest processing, should never be considered as ideal foods."[4]
>
> **Mango Wodzak, Author of *Destination Eden* who also appears in the film *Pure Fruit***

Destination Eden is the first book I read which deals with the ethical and spiritual nature of fruitarianism and how fruits will fundamentally lead us to the Garden of Eden. We can clearly see that in The Bible, Adam and Eve partook in the sacred religion of eating fruits, nourishing themselves. Fruits symbolize unconditional love for all of nature and the creatures. The wolf sat beside the lamb in peaceful coexistence; everything was in harmony until after the apple was eaten. After that time, we started looking at other plants and then animals as food sources. Later, when we started herding animals, we started seeing women as property, existing only to serve man and blacks as slaves only to serve whites.

In the Garden of Eden, there are no fishing operations, animal farms or destructive monocultures of grain. In the Garden of Eden no petrochemicals exist; there is no violence of any sort, theft, fear or hatred towards anyone. The Garden of Eden is a place of love and compassion for all.

Endless hours are spent preparing and cooking food, there is energy waste from the cooking process, the never-ending list continues. Fruit is fast food, freeing up time to engage in healthy pursuits. All one may need is a knife and a spoon. Some fruits, such as apples, pears, bananas and oranges can be eaten very easily without any utensils at all.

As gathering Homo sapiens who foraged for fruit, we came upon a fruit tree and devoured their sweets until we were satiated. I imagine that in the past, we lived in search of fruit trees upon fruit trees, eating mono meals until we were satisfied. We are not the hunters or scavengers that we think we were. This type of living started when the abundance of fruits started to diminish. No one knows why the fruit supply ever became scarce. There could have been a flood or some storm that caused the destruction of the food around us.

Now, supermarkets carry all sorts of processed and refined foods in packages, bottles and cans that also need huge amounts of petrochemicals to produce. It takes huge machines, heat and other equipment to process the food even further, making packaged food one of the ultimate destructions to the earth.[5] And where do the packaging materials go? Some of them are recycled and turned into new plastic or other materials, but most items that are not recycled end up in landfills or oceans. Surprisingly, a lot of packages cannot be recycled due to contamination.[6] This is devastating.

In India, cattle inevitably consume plastics and other debris as they walk along the streets and onto the landfills. Autopsies show that pounds of garbage end up in the stomachs of cattle.[7]

With all this destruction, how can we ever expect to live in The Garden of Eden? Even as a vegan, one contributes to some suffering and harm. Of course, there is not any lifestyle that does not cause harm, but we must strive to cause the least harm possible. In The Garden of Eden, there are no rice fields, no veggie burgers or soy milk trees. If we ever want to live in peace, we need to attempt to do the least harm possible. Fruits play a vital role in all this. As more and more of us see the vital role that fruits play in shaping this world, we will start transforming our world into the Garden of Eden that we all pray for.

A Better way to Live

There is a better way to live. We have to do the best we can. Not everyone will be inclined to eat only fruits at every meal for their entire lives, or move to the tropics and live like nomads. Even though soy burgers and rice fields are not as environmentally friendly as fruit orchards are, they are much friendlier to the farm animals that are tortured and slaughtered for food for consumption.

Veganism is a start to a new life, but it is not the end. Once we understand the ethical and spiritual motivations of veganism we must embody veganism in our daily lives. We must elevate our consciousness to a new level, to include more raw food until we get to fruitarianism.

If one does not think they have the will power to get there, then that is fine, but the more we eat from the Garden of Eden, the faster we will get there. That is why Freelee's *Raw till 4* program is great for a lot of people who cannot give up cooked meals entirely.[8] I tend to do this when I absolutely cannot find too many good fruits or do not have much ripe fruit around. Again, do the best you can and strive for Eden.

Do the Best you can!

I believe everyone can be vegan in today's world. There is no excuse for continuing to rape and torture the earth and kill its innocent beings. I hope the earlier chapters have sparked some awareness about the plight of animals raised for food and the detrimental effects they have on the world. Though I cannot force anyone to live a vegan lifestyle, I hope one day we will live in a more harmonious, Eden-like paradise and I wish to be around to witness it.

If we still believe there must be a better way to raise animals or think that non-human animals do not matter, that is because we have not awakened the empathy in ourselves. Visiting a slaughterhouse or factory farm is a step in the right direction. Think about this, we do not take children to slaughterhouses, but we do take them to pick apples, isn't this strange? Why doesn't McDonald's show their customers where their burgers really come from?

Once we embrace the vegan lifestyle, remember, we must do the best that we can. If all we can do is to purchase conventionally grown produce or eat white rice, then by all means we should do so. Animals will still love us for it. But if we have the time and money to relocate and buy or grow organic produce (better yet, veganically grown produce) or have the willpower to eat more raw food, do so. We absolutely have no time to lose.

We can create a world at peace if we want it. Heaven is here. Heaven is in all of us. But we need to do more than just be vegan or eat more raw food. We need to spread the message far and wide. Even if people criticize or call us all sorts of names, like extremist or radical, we need to be strong in our convictions. We must sing our tune and bring peace to Earth! For the sake of ourselves, Mother Earth and the poor defenceless creatures whom we share this world with.

CHAPTER SEVENTEEN
THE JOURNEY TO COMPASSIONATE CHOICES

Ever since I was a little child I have always loved animals. In my heart I knew I wanted to protect them, however, I was acting contrary to this by eating them. For me, there was a disconnect between my dinner plate and animals. I loved my dog and cat but ate the chicken for dinner.

I loved chicken, hamburgers and hotdogs, cheese, eggs, and seafood. Pure and simple, I just loved the taste. Consciously, in my heart, I knew I was doing something terribly wrong. Subconsciously, in my mid to late teens, I would order mostly vegetarian options in restaurants. I guess that the guilt of consuming murdered animals got me eating mostly vegetarian.

In 2001/2002, I lived with my sister for a brief period while going to school. She claimed to be a vegetarian. She confronted me one day about my eating habits and I told her: "But I like it, I like it. Leave me alone!" She told me about the cruelty to animals, but I would not listen to her. I was closed off, with my blinders on, continuing to eat the foods that I loved. Ever since that time, she never talked to me about vegetarianism.

In 2003, I became interested in documentary films. I loved wild animals and the planet, so I studied all I could. I finally realized I too wanted to create documentary films.

I knew, after watching films like State of the Planet with David Attenborough, that humans were destroying the planet. "How can humans be so cruel and destructive?" I thought to myself. It was not until I saw the remarkable film Sharkwater in 2007 that I started on the path that I still follow today. Sharkwater is a film which speaks of the shark finning industry and the human destruction of the oceans. In 2008, after watching a few animal farming and slaughterhouse undercover videos, I finally gave up eating animal flesh, though I still included seafood, cheese, and eggs in my diet. For some particular reason, I went pescetarian for health reasons. The videos did not have an effect on me ethically though they did plant a seed.

How I Gave up Milk

As a child, I had terrible ear infections and mucus. My mother used an ancient cure on me: warm vegetable oil in the ear, which was always a temporary relief. Today, I believe this was one of the causes of my decline in hearing. I later found out, during my research, that the phlegm (or mucus) was mostly due to milk consumption and that many young children were succumbing to the same problems.[1] It is estimated that three-quarters of the world's adult population is lactose-intolerant because they cannot digest the main sugar in milk, lactose.[2] My mom recommended that I switch to soy milk. So eventually, after her nagging a few times, I did. However, because she purchased the non-sweetened variety I gagged and refused to drink it. Later in my life I tried other flavours of soy and other senon-dairy milks and made the switch.

The Spiritual Awakening

One day, in the spring of 2009, my mom prepared delicious pasta with shrimp sauce. This was about to change my life forever. I suffered food poisoning from this meal and was taken to the hospital. I thought I had contracted swine flu, but in fact it was an extreme case of food poisoning brought on by the shrimp. The doctors did not tell me this, but I knew instinctively it was the shrimp I had eaten. As I lay in the hospital bed, throwing up from time to time, I kept wondering if this was the way we were supposed to live. So many questions were going through my mind, questions I had been trying to answer for years. A few times in my life, I asked my mom those same questions, "What is the reason for life?" and "Why are we born?" She always gave the same answer: "I do not know".

A few weeks after the tragic experience, I was looking out the window meditating, looking up at the sky and my consciousness asked me a question. "If I profess to lc animals and the planet, how could I still be committing such violence by consuming them?" I asked myself. I was a hypocrite. I knew right then that if I truly loved animals and wanted to help protect them the only logical solution was to stop eating them altogether. At first I was scared because I did not know what was happening. I did not want to experience it, but I did, and there was nothing I could do to stop it. A moment later I felt this exuberant feeling come over me. It was the most beautiful thing I have ever felt. It felt as if a weight was being lifted off my shoulders. I felt connected to birds, to trees, the sky, insects and all the creation.

When I stopped consuming animal products I did not understand what vegan meant, even though I heard people using the word. I looked in the dictionary and was still puzzled. I thought vegetarian and vegan were the same. As I did a little more research I finally understood the philosophy of veganism. Today, more than ever, I continue researching and learning about veganism and raw veganism. I continue learning about the ethical and spiritual dimensions of the lifestyle, as well as the environmental and health aspects.

It was not until about a year later that I gave up honey and started donating my animal clothing. I could not bear the thought of wearing or eating anything that came from an animal or just that I was using another creature for their products. It took me years, but I am proud to say that today I am totally animal-free. I feel proud of something I should have done decades ago. I feel proud of what veganism stands for, but most importantly, I feel proud of not harming another being for my pleasures.

Honey

Honey is a sweet food made by bees using nectar from flowers. It is regurgitated food from their stomachs.[3] It can be called stolen bee vomit. Honey is not a plant, nor made by plants and should therefore not be considered vegan. In any case, even if I rarely consumed honey or used bee-derived products, I knew I was still dependent on the use and exploitation of animals. To me, it was not necessary to consume anything that came from or was produced by bees. I felt like a hypocrite, not living the true meaning of veganism, which seeks to do – as far and as wide as possible – the least harm to animals and the earth.

No matter, if it is cruel or not, bees and other animals are not offering their products to us freely. This is the key. As human beings, we must understand what and where our true purpose lies. Use our intuition and live an authentic spiritual life. If we get something from others, it is because they gave it to us and consent to do so. Nonhuman animals do not consent to give us their products or bodies at all. Also, there is no real way to take products from animals that do not harm them in the process. For example, when we take honey from bees (even backyard beekeepers) a lot of bees will defend their hive. Sometimes the bees need to defend themselves, and bees will die when they sting another human or animal. When we steal their honey they do not have any food to feed themselves, especially during the winter months, so the producers usually give bees honey substitute which is sugar water. Sugar water is not a healthy substitute for them. Also the last thing we need to understand is, in order to thrive we do not need to consume anything that comes from an animal. Just think about it, if someone stole our food, or babies or clothes or whatever, we would scream, run away or try to fight back. This is what is happening to bees and other animals.

As a vegan, I see all animals as living creatures like myself; I see them as wanting to live free, away from violence, and in peace and harmony with the rest of creation. I see the trees, the soil and the insects, birds and all other life forms working in harmony with one another. And the truly beautiful people cultivating and growing crops to nourish themselves and help feed a hungry world makes me cry with so much love and joy. I am very blessed to be able to experience living on this magical planet we call home. I know that every time I make a purchase, every time I sit down to eat and every time I celebrate with friends, I am contributing to a better world for future generations and I know that no one suffers and dies needlessly for my choices. I know that with every bite and every choice I make, I am helping feed a hungry world, I am creating more ethical jobs for those in underprivileged countries; and that with my choices, I am restoring nature to what it once was, and by promoting veganism, I am healing the sickness in everyone's bodies, as cholesterol and saturated fat stop eating our hearts away.

My Extreme Family

> "What kind of messed-up brainwashed society are we living in, where exploitation and killing are considered *normal* whereas compassion and non-violence are considered *extreme*?"[4]
> **Mango Wodzak, Author of *Destination Eden* who also appears in the film *Pure Fruit***

At the time I went vegan I was living with my mother, and she somewhat knew why I was vegan. She saw the videos and read the books, but that did not stop her from calling me a fanatic or extremist once in a while. My sister and I would get into arguments on the phone about my extreme vegan lifestyle. She was claiming to be vegetarian, but still consumed seafood, cheese, and eggs. Fish are not plants; they feel pain just like other animals.[5] My sister's reasoning was just like everyone else's in our society. She did not think that fish were sentient and considered vegans to be extremists. At the time, we had these conversations I was still learning how to tackle these arguments. When these discussions were brought forth to me by total strangers, I could easily and rationally discuss them, unlike when I spoke of the same concerns with my family or coworkers.

My sister always uses the argument *vegans are extremists*. How can vegans be extremists when they are the ones who deeply care for animals and Mother Earth? We are the ones who are trying to stop mass deforestation, end world hunger, stop cruelty and clean the air, water, and earth. We are the ones who are trying to stop wars, eliminate diseases and teach others about compassion and love. We are doing all these things as peacefully and as compassionately as we possibly can. Will Tuttle, PhD, author of *The World Peace*

Diet points out, "I think the core of the teaching is really to, spread a sense of radical inclusion and to include everyone in our sphere of compassion."[6] And that is precisely what we are trying to do, to include everyone in our sphere of compassion.

Does the definition of unconditional love exclude animals, nature or the humans who have to do all the slaughtering? Being kind to all life is not a fanatical or extreme idea. It only seems extreme because very few people in our society are living this way.

My Mom and Her Veganish Ways

My mom never really understood veganism until recently, during the last few years of my living with her. I would get her to watch films like *Earthlings* and *Peaceable Kingdom*.[7, 8] But I guess she got misconstrued ideas from her sister about happy animals on family farms. She would drive up north and see cows happily grazing in the fields and thought nothing bad of it. Maybe she thought the undercover footage that she saw (that came from the US) never took place in Canada. This is far from the truth.

Every day I would hound her, explaining the process of modern animal production and showing her videos and she agreed, but she always seemed to end up discussing the idyllic family farm and how animals were treated there. It was her sister who would tell her about her purchases of family-farm, fresh eggs where they let their chickens live out their natural lives. I would argue with her for months on end after learning from people such as Will Tuttle and his book *The World Peace Diet* and Judy Carman's *Peace to all Beings*.[9, 10] Like these authors, I finally started living by example. I thought to myself, it is not doing me or animals any good consistently arguing or preaching to my family about the issue, so I focused on people who were openly willing to learn.

In December 2011, I released my first self-published book, *The Journey to Compassionate Living* and dedicated it to my mother. I gave her the book and she was very proud of me for such an accomplishment. I think she was flabbergasted that I dedicated the book to her. Later, at a party that my mom was also attending, a friend of mine asked me if my mom was vegan. Ever since she read my book I had wondered that myself, but for some reason was afraid to ask. So I posed the question to her later that night and she replied, "I am near vegan". And I was very happy to hear that. Recently she stated that she was 'eighty percent vegan,' and even though I know there is no such as thing as an 'eighty-percent vegan;' either you're vegan or you're not, it is still a big improvement compared to her recent years.

The Problem with Veganish Lifestyles

I think the problem with people who like to call themselves *veganish* or *near vegan*, is that even though they somewhat understand the cruelty in farms and slaughterhouses, they do not seem to understand the implications of consuming foods that contain animal ingredients or are animal tested. Though they may be mostly vegan at home and use egg substitutes or soy milk instead of animal products in baked goods, substituting faux deli meats for turkey or chicken slices in their sandwiches, they purchase bread, pastries, cosmetics, creams or cleaning products that contain animal ingredients or are animal tested.

What they do not understand is that they are still contributing to massive amounts of animal suffering while doing this. Even if the product contains small amounts of animal ingredients, it equals tremendous suffering for animals and Mother Earth. In supermarkets and stores worldwide, many products contain at least one or more animal ingredients, causing animals, humans and the earth to suffer greatly as a result.

Because of corporations and scientific terminology, most people today do not really know what they are buying, even when the package lists the ingredients.

And this is what is happening to millions of other people around the world. Because of the so-called 'labelling laws' and large animal abusing industries and corporations, authorities tend to hide certain information from people. Ingredients are labelled using scientific terms and in certain circumstances, ingredients are written using numbers and words that are extremely long and hard to pronounce. Some plant ingredients may be genetically modified to contain genes from animal origin. No one knows, because it is not required to label these facts (at least not in Canada).[11]

I think the trouble is the hassle of getting to know all the animal ingredients that stop people from going vegan. If there was a cow or chicken's face on the packaging, or if the product plainly stated what was in it, it would get people thinking twice. But because we are so familiar with certain products that are packaged nicely and disguised in plastic or in a bottle or container, we never think about the cruelty behind these products. Whey is known as "the watery liquid that remains when milk forms curds", l-cysteine is "an amino acid from hair which can come from human hair, hog hair or duck feathers" and any of the following derivative names: stearic acid, stearyl betaine, stearyl imidazoline, stearamide, stearamine, stearamine oxide, stearates, stearic hydrazide, stearone, stearoxytrimethylsilane and stearoyl lactylic acid is "fat from cows and sheep and from dogs and cats euthanized in animal shelters, etc. and most often refers to a fatty substance taken from the stomachs of pigs".[12] These and other scientific names are never labelled with their real animal name such as *whale oil,* but with their scientific name. However in today's society, more and more, foods are labelled as *vegan* that are truly animal free. They are popping up everywhere, including national grocery chains and smaller ones as well.

I am very happy with the way I have influenced my mother to transition to veganism. Even though she is not truly vegan, it is this *near vegan* lifestyle that will eventually lead her, and others, down the path to higher consciousness. I do believe that one day, she will become fully vegan, just like I believe in the day when the world will become vegan.

I have faith in the impossible, because nothing is really impossible to achieve. People believe it is not possible to get the world to go vegan in one's lifetime, so they educate people on the meagre little changes that they believe people can make. They promote the welfare of tortured and slaughtered animals, family farms, etc., praising this lifestyle like they are doing no harm. I think such an approach is very harmful to the animal advocacy movement. It sends a message to people that we can continue using, exploiting and killing animals for food and other purposes.

My mother has asked me many times why I always watch the awful cruelty videos. I did not know how to answer her at the time, but after hearing Will Tuttle mention in one of his interviews, "If the animals are going through it, I want to know what it is." it got me thinking. It is not that I actually like watching the cruelty videos; I just have to know what animals are going through. It motivates me to want to do more for them. I think everyone needs to see these ghastly images.

When we start addressing our relationship with animals, we will start seeing the best in humanity. Once we start addressing the issue and seeing animals not merely as commodities but as sentient beings that have the right to live freely of humans, we will start witnessing a positive transformation in our lives and will be able to help the world around us.

I do not think we could ever live peacefully as omnivores on this planet even if we raised animals differently. Even if, theoretically, we were to replace factory farming with small-scale, family farming, it would still be totally absurd. It would not be possible in today's society, eating the vast quantities of animal products we do. Family farms would not be able to sustain our big appetite for animal food. We would not be able to kill the numbers of animals that we do today without somehow compromising animal welfare standards. We would still need to mercilessly kill animals anyways. In the end, innocent beings die needlessly.

My Aunt and Her Family Farming Ideas

My aunt told me that when she was a child, her family used to raise cows for their milk. Most of the milk would be given to her baby and the rest would be given to her family. She claims they had to take some of the milk because the mother cow was producing too much of it. This seems very unbelievable. Just like other mammals, cows produce just enough milk for their baby and their baby only.[13] To say that the cow was producing too much milk is absurd, unless her family was forcing the cow to produce more milk than she would naturally. Also, let's not forget that the mother has to be impregnated to produce milk. What happens to the calves when they are born? Almost always, even on smaller dairy farms, the calf is stolen from her mother and is either killed right away, put into veal production or, if the calf is female, put into herself production.[14] Because my aunt was very young at the time, and it was many decades ago, she could not possibly remember the exact process. Her parents told her what they wanted her to believe. She can continue justifying the practise, but in any case, as Will Tuttle, PhD mentioned in an interview,

> "Even animal foods, no matter where they come from, whether it is hunting, I mean hunting is probably the least harmful, but as soon as we own animals, as soon as we have any sense of ownership, property. Owning another being is violence. Actually it is a delusion; we do not own another living being."[15]

There is a short, two-minute video of the separation of a mother cow and her calf on a small free range operation.[16] It is one of the most heartbreaking videos I've ever seen. People ask me how milk could be so cruel when they do not kill the cow. The bond between mother and baby is so strong that it lasts well beyond adulthood. Just imagine your baby being taken away from you. How could such a thing ever be done? It is unimaginably the cruellest form of abuse anywhere. The mother cow cries and bellows for days on end for her baby.[17] It is the saddest thing that anyone could ever do.

When we include all animals into our sphere of compassion, we soon start understanding our purpose as human beings. Our purpose is not to accumulate useless possessions, but to give things away. Our purpose is not to dominate other species, but to love and care for them. We are not here to take from the earth, but to give back.

Another important issue that needs to be addressed is the fact that my aunt purchases her eggs from a family farm where they take good care of their animals. Chicken eggs can be considered a direct equivalent to the menstrual cycle in humans.[18] While yes, the caretakers or farmers may take very good care of animals, let's take a closer look at what it entails raising backyard chickens.

Karen Davis, PhD is the author of several books including, Prisoned Chickens, Poisoned Eggs: An Inside Look at the Modern Poultry Industry, More Than a Meal: The Turkey in History, Myth, Ritual, and Reality and Instead of Chicken, Instead of Turkey: A Poultryless 'Poultry' Potpourri. She has written numerous articles on the implications of raising and taking care of backyard chickens for their meat and eggs. She is the founder and president of United Poultry Concerns, a non-profit organization dedicated to the compassionate and respectful treatment of domestic fowl.[19]

She goes on to say,

> "Many suburban chicken-keepers purchase their chickens by mail order from industrial hatcheries. People ordering chickens this way are often surprised at how sickly the birds are, not realizing that the hatchery experience plus the shipping ordeal weakens the birds' immunity, predisposing them to illness and early death. Hatcheries that mass-produce chicks for feed stores and backyard flocks treat the birds and their offspring the way puppy mills treat breeding dogs and their puppies. Since there are no welfare laws regulating these operations, suppliers' website images of green grass, sunny skies, and happy chickens are more likely fictitious than true.
>
> As well as the hatchery experience, airmail shipping takes a toll on the birds' wellbeing. Birds shipped by airmail are often deprived of food and water for up to 72 hours or more, while being exposed to extreme temperatures and rough handling in their shipping crates. Even birds who survive these

traumas and deprivations may be permanently debilitated, particularly if they become dehydrated during long flights and airport layovers. This can lead to the abandonment of hens that don't thrive or are not laying enough eggs to please their purchasers. But this isn't all! Many people are shocked to discover that their order of female chicks includes unwanted roosters in the shipping box. Hatcheries frequently use rooster chicks as packing material - they call them "packers" - regardless of whether male birds were ordered, and chicken sexing is often done incorrectly. Ordinances that permitting chicken-keeping cause purchasers to have to find homes for their unwanted roosters. Because good homes for roosters are very hard to find (most good homes already have as many roosters as they can handle), most roosters end up being turned loose or dumped at shelters, where they are typically killed, having nowhere to go."[20]

Also, she goes on to say,

"The keeping of farm animals attracts rodents and flies. Rats and mice are drawn to the seeds, grains and other feed rations and to the bedding of straw or woodchips for nesting and reproduction. Manure, feed, broken eggs and dripping milk attract flies, and snakes can also move in. The only way to prevent the flies and rodents that normally accompany the keeping of poultry and goats is through undesirable toxic chemicals or by scrupulous cleanliness.

Having run a chicken sanctuary for 25 years, and having dealt with urban backyard chicken-keeping issues around the country, I have learned that many residential owners of chickens do not practice scrupulous or even moderate cleanliness. Most know little or nothing about keeping farm animals, or else they model their practices on standard farming practices and conditions that a suburb would not tolerate. Ignorance is encouraged by claims that farm animals require little labour. This falsehood has led many people to want to keep chickens, goats and other farm animals, thinking they can have a ready supply of animal products with little or no work."[21]

As Karen Davis points out, "Many suburban chicken-keepers purchase their chickens by mail order from industrial hatcheries."[20]

After a few years, the hens are killed anyways because their egg production declines and they are no longer deemed profitable. Whatever the reason, family farmers try convincing consumers that their animals live happy lives, roaming and foraging in the grass, spending time in their natural habitat. While this is true, what they do not tell them is the gruesome story behind it all. No matter if animals are free range, free roaming, organic or 'humanely slaughtered;' they are still killed in gruesome ways, well before their natural lifespan.

As stated by Supreme Master Ching Hai,

"Most eggs produced commercially are unfertilized. The egg remains unfertilized because the appropriate circumstances for its fertilization have been withheld, so the egg cannot complete its natural process of developing into a chicken. Even though this development has not occurred, it still contains the innate life force needed for this. We know that eggs have innate life force; otherwise, why is it that ova are the only type of cells which can be fertilized?"[22]

Another problem with raising animals for their products such as milk or eggs is that we are still dependent on them for their food. We are stealing their products that were intended for them or their babies. When we steal from animals it boomerangs back to us as stealing from other humans. We may not believe this to be so because as humans we have lost the ability to make vital connections and therefore we see humans, animals, and the earth as separate from one another, rather than interconnected.

My Journey Bearing Witness

The time came when the truck was in front of me. As the truck got closer I felt a lump in my throat. Looking out from the ventilation holes were many faces I will never forget. Pigs, innocent and fearful, were drooling, crammed very tightly, some standing on each other, dehydrated and their bodies covered in scratches and bruises. Even though it was just a few moments before the truck would make its way to the slaughterhouse, it was the most heartbreaking moment of my life.

As I was capturing their faces on camera something caught my attention; it was one pig in particular. I could see her loneliness, the suffering and the sadness in her eyes. Something at that moment changed my life forever. The pain she was feeling was the pain I was also feeling. As I gazed into her eyes, she cried out to me, “Why are you doing this to us?” I lowered my camera, crying; I did not know why, but I felt so ashamed that I supported the egregious suffering and consumption of animal products for the first twenty-six years of my life. Looking into the eyes of the innocent animal, she taught me one thing, that I needed to be a guardian for them and that I needed to do more than what I was already doing.

When the truck drove off, I then realized what my purpose was. And I made a promise to the pigs that I would dedicate my life to awakening people to the truth of *the interconnectedness of life*, that is, the unconditional love for all beings, which is to be vegan.

As Leo Tolstoy said,

> "As long as there are slaughterhouses, there will be battlefields."[23]

Throughout the years I've witnessed thousands of pigs, cows and chickens go to slaughter. Each and every one of them is an individual creature wanting to live free and in peace. But, creating peace on Earth cannot take place when we are confining and killing them. As an intelligent society we have to ask ourselves; do we really want to be free? What kind of planet do we want to leave to our children and future generations? Do we want to create a place of violence or a place of peace? Do we want to create a place of abundance for everyone? Do we want to live in a world with clean water, clean food, and clean air? Do we really want to end wars and world hunger? If the answer is yes then the only logical solution is to adopt a vegan lifestyle for the planet, humans and animals. In time, we must enact a massive change if we want to survive on this planet.

> As Will Tuttle PhD, the author of the book *The World Peace Diet* says,
> "I don't think it is far off, I think it is inevitable that we will wake up, that this violence towards animals which boomerangs as violence, disease and a sense of apathy and as low self-esteem in people and basically be enslavement in many ways of humans, would completely change."

For the first twenty-six years of my life, I did not bother connecting animal use, suffering and their murder to the food on my plate, to the clothes that I wore and other uses of animals for testing and entertainment. As intelligent human beings, our purpose is to care for one another with love, kindness, and understanding. We must put others in front of ourselves. As Mahatma Gandhi said, "I must reduce myself to zero and put myself last among [my] fellow creatures."[24] And that is what I myself must do.

As I look back at the first twenty-six years of my life, I was simply living a lie. I was programmed by our culture, thinking that eating animals and their products was a natural, normal, and necessary thing to do. My parents, teachers, and all the forces in my culture taught me that. Not once did I ever question it. It is ingrained in all of us from the time we are infants. And after decades of eating this way, we believe it to be totally normal. Anyone who goes against the status quo is either considered an extremist or a fanatic.

Loving another being is not extreme; it is an altruistic act. When we love, we do not kill and we see killing as morally wrong. When we love, we see everyone as equals, seeing ourselves in another. This is the true pinnacle for human beings.

CHAPTER EIGHTEEN
MY YOUNGER YEARS

Companion Animals

As a young child, I grew up around animals; companion dogs, cats, a hamster, a rabbit, birds, and fish. I remember I was always an animal lover, However, every chance I got, I would consume animal food without ever giving any thought to it. I was acting contrarily for my love of animals. But in my mid-to-late teens I turned sadistic. At that time, I had no idea what I was doing, but deep down in my bones I knew what I was doing was terribly wrong. Every chance I got I would abuse my companion animals. If they did not listen to me I would kick, slap, punch and throw them on the hard, concrete floor. And this would go on for several minutes at a time, for years. I got a thrill every time I abused them; the same exhilarating feeling that slaughterhouse workers experience every time they are around animals. Eventually, my companion animals (especially my dog) were terrified of me. No more would they listen to my commands or even look at me. Every time I came even a tad close to them they would turn away fearfully. I could see the terror in their eyes, and that made me feel sick inside. I knew I needed help, but I was so afraid to face anyone about it.

After those horrible few years of my life, being as sadistic towards animals as I was, I knew I did not want to live this way anymore. I knew I wanted to stop abusing them, but I could not. It was a sickness, and I needed help. During this time, subconsciously, I felt what I was doing was against everything I had ever believed in. I started ordering more vegetarian meals at restaurants, but my addictions for animal foods were ever so much stronger at home. In my late teens, I finally had enough of my animal abusing days. I no longer wanted to be the monster that I was. I convinced myself that I no longer wanted to abuse any animal, so I vowed never to have another pet for as long as I lived. One of my last pets was a dog, an American Eskimo, as white as snow. He was so physiologically and physically abused that he started to defecate all around the house. Because of this, we could not care for him any longer.

To this day, just thinking of my beloved companions and what I did to them makes me weep. The sight of the American Eskimo and the thought of me abusing my beloved companions will never be forgotten. As I write this story, more than a decade later, I mourn for them. How could I have ever done such cruel things, to innocent beings?

Still, even with the way I felt about abusing my own pets I continued eating animal food, not knowing the harm in doing so. Like dogs and cats, farm animals are capable of suffering and feeling pain. I did not make the connection, but later, that changed.

In 2008 when I became a pescetarian after watching the documentary Sharkwater and animal farming and slaughterhouse undercover videos, I did it for health reasons. Even though I saw undercover videos, because of my strong, meat-eating addiction, I did not make the ethical connection to veganism.

The first time I ever heard the word vegan was in the film Shirley Valentine as a teenager. Even though I was not aware of it then, it subconsciously planted a seed in me. Every time I came upon the word it planted more seeds. In 2009, when I started volunteering for animals, again I was confronted with veganism. At that point even though I claimed to be vegetarian, I still consumed the occasional shrimp, cheese, and eggs.

The Circus

The circus is another part of my life that I began to view negatively as I grew older and more sensitive to the plight of animals. Every child grows up loving animals. We have stuffed animal toys as children, books about animals, and we see animals in zoos, but somewhere along the years we disconnect the love of animals with our entertainment choices. On one occasion, I remember going to the circus, but as a youngster I had absolutely no concern for the ridiculous tricks and stunts the animals were taught. I had no worries or guilt. That day I had my picture taken with a bear, feeling very proud. However, years later, after seeing the photograph, I knew that dominating other sentient beings was a terrible act. The bear had a muzzle on him and he was sitting in a chair next to me. No bear in nature would do such a thing. They have to be abused time and time again to be able to perform. I asked my mom, "How on Earth can humans do that to animals?" Still, the answer she gave was, "I do not know."

The Zoo

I have gone to the zoo many times, but the vivid memory of one particular gorilla still sticks in my mind. I saw many times, animals in small cages and enclosures walking and sitting on concrete floors. Their natural habitat is denied to them. While yes, some things in their enclosures were just like you would find in nature, the enclosure is man-made to suit the budgets of the zoo owners and investors and not the interests of animals. Most animals need many hundreds or even thousands of acres to roam around. Zoos are just another place of domination of non-human, living species.

I was looking into the gorilla exhibit and just then, one of them threw up and later ate his own vomit. Many years later, I found that this is a neurological behaviour due to the animal being enclosed in an unnatural setting.[1] It is the same as any animal, human or non-human, living in a cage, pacing back and forth or turning in circles.

Are zoos good educational institutions? No. Putting animals in cages or in small concrete pens is neither good for them nor for us. They sleep on concrete floors, have barely enough room to move and are fed unnatural diets.[2] They are not living the natural lives they were intended to live.

It is proven that most zoo animals live shorter lives compared to their wild ancestors. Most zoos do not provide the public with enough educational information.[2, 3] I like to call these places jail cells for animals. They are just like human jails. Children and even adults are seen going to these places and instead of learning about animals, they laugh, ridicule and treat them like trash. This is neither considered educational nor intelligent on our part.

In our culture, I do not think we ever question anything that we are taught. Things are just as is and we do not question them. My mom, like the rest of us, was taught from a young age exactly what her parents and teachers thought she should know. For decades, we have been victims of this same cultural indoctrination.

I was taught that all this was normal from a young age. My mom, innocent like the rest of us, grew up thinking that this was how we were supposed to live and she passed the teaching down to me. I was taught that what was on TV was real, what we buy in the supermarkets is healthy, what the doctors told us would fix our illnesses and what our governments said was the truth. This is far from reality. Until we start questioning everything that our culture has taught us, we will never solve any of our man-made dilemmas. We need to question our health care system, public school systems, governments, taxes, laws, our food and municipal water. We have to question everything. Until we do we will never live in a harmonious and loving society.

Questioning Everything

As a teenager and young adult, I questioned everything. I wondered if this was the way we were supposed to live. I did not understand why there was so much violence all around us; why humans were destroying the environment and how we were disrespectful to animals. I started meditating as a young adult, trying to understand. I saw documentary films and did research on the Internet, but I just could not understand. Though I always went back to the photo of the bear in the muzzle beside me at the circus and wondered, how on Earth could anyone commit such atrocity to an innocent creature? And funny enough, there I was consuming animal products without a single worry in the world. I did not understand that I was the problem and that I needed to change my habits.

Back in 2009 when I had the revelation, I went to look at the photo of the bear and I asked myself, "How on Earth did we ever get to this point?" My heart was broken and I knew I was the one that had to be the solution. And finally, everything came together. I knew that in order for life to survive on Earth we had to stop eating and using animals. That was the only way to save humanity. It was that simple.

But how was I going to tell everyone? Everyone loved their bacon and eggs and cheeseburgers. Why would anyone want to listen to me? And then it hit me. While I was looking at the photograph, I knew inside me that the Universe needed my help. I had this revelation that I was to live a very long time and help animals and the planet. I could not believe it. It was the most beautiful thing I have ever felt. I finally was given a gift; I found my purpose in life. This all happened the first time I had the awakening. The entire experience gave me goose bumps, a feeling of joy.

A few weeks later I started organizing demonstrations, which only my mom and I attended. Eventually, for some reason or another, I went into a state of depression for a couple of years because I knew that everything could not change overnight. And to this day I am so thankful and happy with my life.

In 2011, when I started volunteering with grassroots organizations and bearing witness of animals in trucks destined for the slaughterhouse, I knew once again that I needed to do more for them. Even though I started writing this book in 2010, ever since bearing witness to animals, I knew there was an emergency, and that I had to increase my workload. At the end of 2012 I left my day job to work on my book full-time, along with the film in 2013.

I always tell people to question everything. When we start questioning everything we were once taught we start opening our hearts to all the suffering around us. When we witness all the suffering around us, we will want to make the world a better place. And when we try to make the world around us better, we will start witnessing suffering and negativity as positive and beauty. If we want to live in the Garden of Eden, we must bring The Garden of Eden to Earth. How can we create a world of peace when our minds are clouded with erroneous childhood teachings?

School systems around the world teach us only what they want us to learn. Propaganda and advertising from animal and chemical corporations make it even harder for us to break through this ignorance. It is time that we awaken to the reality. Indeed, there are alternatives to today's education system. Homeschooling is a good choice. It is an alternative to the modern-day public school system.[4] Another alternative is to leave modern-day life altogether and live like nomads out in nature. Of course, most of us will never leave society for nature, but gradually we can remove the toxic programming and materialism from our lives one day at a time.

When we question society, we are going against the grain. In reality, we are not fighting or going against anyone, we are just sharing our message of unconditional love for all beings. When we see our movement as one of peace, loving and caring for others, no longer will we see negativity or suffering around us.

In reality there is no opposition [i.e. us against the SAD, animal-eating capitalists], there is only a cognitive dissonance and apathy on their part. Once we love everyone, negativity and hate start to fall apart. As vegans, we cannot hate anyone. There is no hate, violence or prejudices against anyone, not even against slaughterhouse workers, CEOs of multi-national corporations, political systems or governments. Why? The definition of unconditional love means just that: "affection without any limitations" or "love without conditions".[5] Therefore, we must love everyone, no matter the circumstance. We must even love our worst enemies. Unconditional love does not mean that we hate our enemies, it means we must love them, just as we must love ourselves.

Questioning everything our culture has taught us, I believe, is a step in the right direction. Once we start witnessing all the suffering around us we can begin to do something about it. Once we stop seeing animals as property to be used and become vegan educators, our lives will be beautiful.

I now understand why I abused animals and how it directly relates to eating them and their products. When we consume their bodies and secretions we take in their suffering, abuse, torture, boredom, depression, death etc. There is a direct correlation between farm animal abuse and domestic abuse of companion animals, spousal, and child.

Animals have suffered tremendously under our domination; isn't it about time they have the right to their lives and their freedom?

CHAPTER NINETEEN
OTHER ISSUES

Tobacco

Smoking (especially cigarettes) is practised by around 1.22 billion people worldwide.[1] It causes lung disease, oesophagus, kidney, and bladder cancer, bronchitis, emphysema, heart disease, stroke, and impotence.[2] There are 599 additives in the average brand of cigarettes and more than 7000 chemical compounds are created by burning cigarettes. Out of the 7000 chemicals found in cigarettes, 250 are poisonous.[3]

Pharmaceuticals

Pharmaceutical drugs and animal food work hand in hand. When we eat animal food, we will need medication. Factory farmed animals are given tons of antibiotics and medication because they are cramped in filthy living conditions. Their respiratory system breaks down and cannot cope with these conditions, resulting in various illnesses to the eyes, skin and lungs. As a result, when we eat their products, our bodies develop similar symptoms; we then take medications and antibiotics to cure them.[4]

If we eat a healthy diet of fruit and vegetables, there would not be a need for pharmaceutical medications or even Tylenol. A healthy diet, combined with daily exercise, good sleep and hydration is essential for a vital, functioning body.

Alcohol

One glass of red wine is touted for its natural powers for decreasing heart disease, but that is only because of the grapes in the wine. Fruits, vegetables, whole grains and legumes will fill you up and there are no side effects. According to Supreme Master Television, alcohol takes the lives of 1.8 million people worldwide annually.[5] Even in small quantities, consumed over decades, alcohol can increase the risk for certain cancers, liver, and cardiovascular disease.[6, 7] It can even lead to brain damage (amnesia, dementia and brain shrinkage), and organ failures in the heart, liver, kidney, stomach, pancreas, and eyes. Alcohol is also the cause of a multitude of birth defects such as mental retardation, Fetal Alcohol Syndrome, stunted growth, facial deformity, Sudden Infant Death Syndrome and miscarriage.[8]

According to Neal Barnard, MD, from his book Breaking the Food Seduction, even one drink of alcohol increases the risk of breast and colon cancer. Even the short term effects are very negative, alcohol is known to cause intoxication and dehydration.[8] Low to medium alcohol consumption (such as a glass of wine a day) has some minor health benefits; however, the minor health benefits are outweighed by the negative health effects.

Caffeine

Decaffeinated coffee still includes some caffeine.[9] Various soft drinks, energy drinks, foods, and medications also include caffeine.[10,11] Most kinds of tea include caffeine, except for herbal tea which usually does not.[12] Caffeine is a natural substance found in the leaves, seeds and fruits of certain plants. Some studies suggest that moderate consumption of caffeine is harmful, while others do not. Caffeine can cause tiredness, nervousness, irritability, insomnia and mood swings. It can also cause stomach ulcers and heart palpitations.[13-15]

Caffeine is usually needed in one's diet because the body's adrenals are exhausted. This is due to one or more of the following reasons: not following a healthy diet of predominantly raw fresh fruit and vegetables, dehydration, insufficient sleep, lack of exercise or a combination of all the above.

Cacao

Cacao also spelled cocoa, is a fermented bean coming from the theobroma cacao tree, or simply cacao tree.[16] I myself used to consume at least $50 CAD worth of milk chocolate every week. I used to consume extreme amounts of chocolate until I threw up. I was that addicted. And that is what chocolate is, addicting. Few are able to consume a small amount; we need to eat the whole thing in order to be satisfied. In fact, most people who do not eat a healthy diet of mainly raw fruits and vegetables tend to get their daily fix from caffeinated products such as coffee or chocolate. According to Jeremy Saffron, one of the first people to promote cacao, "Because it [cacao] doesn't have any major health benefits. I mean minor health benefits, just like alcohol has minor health benefits."[17]

The cacao bean, including the leaves of tea plants, kola (or cola) nut and guarana berry, holly berries, Ilex guayusa and Ilex paraguariensis (yerba mate), contain theobromine, which is a neurotoxin.[18] In small quantities, chocolate does not have any major side effects, however in large quantities, over time, it can lead to theobromine poisoning and have effects on the liver, kidneys and the adrenals. Chocolate or cacao can also cause mood swings and it is a known carcinogen raw or cooked, it is known to cause cancer in animals, especially dogs that usually die after consuming it. An alternative to cacao is carob. Carob does not have the side effects like cacao does and it contains virtually no theobromine (0.000–0.504 mean theobromine content ratio), whereas cacao can have as much as 20.3.[19-21]

During the production of cacao, on the Ivory Coast, the world's largest producer of cacao, some 200,000 child slave labourers with some 12,000 of them having been abducted from their families are forcefully employed. They work up to twelve-hour days, are beaten regularly and most are working with pesticides without any protective equipment. More than sixty percent of them are children under the ages of fourteen and forty percent of the children are girls.[22-24] The Dark Side of Chocolate is a great documentary film examining this issue.[25]

Sweatshops

Sweatshop is a term used to describe factories where workers rights are violated. They work long hours in low-paying jobs where they may be routinely beaten; they have little to no rights. Amongst them are women and child labourers, some of them abducted or bought from their families.[26, 27]

Slavery was abolished in the United States under the Thirteenth Amendment to the United States Constitution in December, 1865.[28] Yet even to this day, according to various organizations, an estimated twenty to thirty-six million slaves still exist in the world.[29]

It was not until 1893 that women were given the right to vote in New Zealand, and 1902 in Australia.[30, 31] It was not until after World War I that women were given the vote in the USA, Canada, and Britain.[32-34] In 1929, in Canada, the five Lords of the Committee ruled unanimously that "the word 'persons' in Section 24 includes both the male and female sex." They called the earlier interpretation "a relic of days more barbarous than ours."[35]

The Bottom Line

If we are dependent on energy drinks, medications, tobacco, chocolate or even coffee or tea, it means we are not eating healthy, sleeping well, exercising and hydrating ourselves. There is not even a single animal that consumes these products, therefore we should not either. Even though there may be minor health benefits to using these products, the negative side effects always outweigh them.

All of us can choose a more compassionate lifestyle, and create a world where all humans are free from slavery and can earn a decent living. It is with our buying power that we can do this. When we buy fair trade products such as coffee, bananas or cacao, we put our ethics on the table. In a society where corporations rule, it is hard to be totally ethical. But by understanding the power of sweatshop-free products (the products with the fair trade logo), we understand that we can live in a world free of human slavery.

CHAPTER TWENTY
STORIES OF COMPASSION

A Biologist's Journey to Veg
By Jonathan Balcombe, PhD

Story used with the permission of Dr. Mary Clifton and Jonathan Balcombe

Jonathan Balcombe, PhD is the Department Chair for Animal Studies with Humane Society University. He is the author of *Pleasurable Kingdom: Animals and the Nature of Feeling Good, Second Nature: The Inner Lives of Animals,* and *The Exultant Ark: A Pictorial Tour of Animal Pleasure.* He has been vegan since 1989.

I've always considered myself to have been a vegetarian waiting to happen. According to my mother, I was five years old [when] she started giving me meat. So "born-again vegetarian" might describe the decision I made at age 24 to go "on the carrot," as one of my mentors at the time derisively put it. From my earliest memories I've had a burning curiosity about animals and a deep concern for their welfare. My first career ambition, at age four, was to become either a postman or a hippopotamus. The inspiration for the latter came from family visits to the London Zoo, where I watched fascinated as the affectionately-named hippo, Nada the Lily, would open her enormous gape to receive a whole fresh cabbage from the keeper. With a series of massive chomps, Nada would reduce the cabbage to mush—rivulets of cabbage juice streaming through pink channels before sluicing down her throat. Restrictions on feeding the animals were more lax in the early 1960s, and Nada would readily accept various tidbits tossed to her from the public standing overhead. I remember a piece of popcorn, lobbed in by some unusually optimistic bystander, getting hopelessly lost in the complex landscape of Nada's oral cavity. Knowing what I now know of the monotonous, often lonely existence of so many animals confined to zoos, I would have changed my mind about being a hippo. Popcorn was probably one of the brighter spots in Nada's days.

The catalyst for my starting to eat animals and for my stopping again was, in both cases, overseas travel. When I was three, my adventurous parents decided to move half way round the world, from England to New Zealand. With over a dozen sheep for every human, New Zealand at that time ranked first in the world (or last, from the animals' perspective) in per capita meat consumption. So it was perhaps inevitable that my parents—unsteeped in the moral arguments for vegetarianism that have since matured—capitulated to local custom and began to put mutton and lamb on the table. Never a fussy eater, I took to these new tastes with gusto. I still recall as a boy sucking the grease and fat from the "crackling" following a pork roast, and sneaking into the kitchen to find the chewy bacon rinds left over from breakfast.

Twenty years on, when I decided to take a year off university biology studies to save some money and go on an overseas adventure, I was well on the way to going veg. For humanitarian reasons I had shunned veal, and whenever there was a meatless option at my college dorm cafeteria, I took it. But I knew the taste of Big Macs, Whoppers, and Filet-o'-Fish sandwiches, and I ordered half-chicken dinners at Swiss Chalet restaurants. When I discovered cooking at age 22, my favourite dish was spaghetti Bolognese with plenty of ground beef fried up with diced onions and green peppers.

I chose India for my next travel destination. My mother's best friend was Indian, and I had acquired a taste for Indian cuisine from visits to their Toronto home, where their live-in cook, brought over from the family's lavish Mumbai home, prepared delectable feasts. Like some half-billion Indian Hindus, the Mehta's are vegetarian. Going to India not only meant I would have a congenial home base in Mumbai (Bombay then), but exploring the country's plant-based diet would be a cinch. By the time I'd purchased the airline tickets for a three month stay, I'd decided to take the tofu plunge.

Looking back, I shake my head when I think that it took me twenty years to return to my vegetarian beginnings.

Today, the idea of eating meat is as alien to me as India was when I arrived there in January 1984. It was 5 a.m., and Mumbai's airport was already bustling. As jet-lagged travelers shuffled towards stern-faced immigration officials, a tiny barefooted woman swept the floors with a primitive straw whisk, and a scrawny, pregnant cat foraged in the garbage receptacles. Hours later, as a ragged amputee begged at the window of my taxi, I felt the tightening grip of culture-shock, and longed to catch the next flight home.

Ten days on, somewhat acclimated to urban India's constant assault on the senses, I set off to explore the hinterland. Traveling alone in India was challenging and never dull. I soon learned to purchase fruit through the train windows from the inevitable vendors at each station. I peeled mangoes and guavas with my penknife, heeding the health advisories to avoid anything that might have been washed in Indian water. My travels to nature reserves took me well off the beaten track. At a rural bus-stop, a small gathering of villagers stared wide-eyed at me as though I'd just emerged from a flying saucer. But "all-veg" restaurants were never far away. I soon discovered the vegetarian Thai, a smorgasbord of native dishes arrayed in shiny metal bowls and served on a large metal tray accompanied by a generous heap of rice. Indians traditionally eat with their right hand (the left is reserved for private hygiene), so these meals usually arrived without cutlery. My subsequent request usually yielded a spoon that looked more suitable for feeding a mouse. But the meals were invariably satisfying, scrumptious and criminally inexpensive.

My one foray off the carrot was in November 1985 when I traveled with a research team to South Africa for a month, studying bats in Kruger Park. Our encampment on the Luvuvhu River was staffed by two black servant-cooks. Our evening meals resembled something from an Atherosclerotics Anonymous cookbook: a red meat centerpiece and a large dollop of sudsa—South Africa's answer to cream-of-wheat—doused in heavy gravy. Any vegetable that made it onto the plate huddled nervously at the rim, stared down by a menacing slab of someone's former shoulder or thigh.

Nature found a creative way to reprimand me for my waywardness. Two weeks into the trip, I became someone else's meal. During a daytime bat tracking foray, I noticed that a scattering of insect bites on my chest were becoming itchier. Squinting down for a closer look, I realized that one of the little red welts was…moving! Two hours later, with the help of strategically-applied Vaseline, I squeezed four oxygen-starved, rice-grain-sized maggots from my torso. Our South African guide just happened to be an authority on parasitic flies. He informed me that my dinner guests were African skin maggots (*Cordylobia anthropophaga*, translation: eater of men), a species not previously reported this far south. So, an erstwhile vegetarian had assisted the range expansion of a fellow meat-eater.

I remember in 1991 having an argument with a fellow biologist on the matter of whether or not human dentition had evolved for meat. I contended that because our teeth are bunodont (a term I had learnt in a mammalogy course and now deployed to try to impress or intimidate my older adversary) and because they also lack the long canines and tearing carnassials (take that!) of meat-eaters, our teeth were meant for eating fruits, nuts and other plant-based foods. Lacking that basic skill of argumentation which says "listen to the other guy," I don't recall his main points. It was a rather pointless exchange, for humans evolved neither as vegetarians nor carnivores. Humans are omnivores. Our teeth and intestines are those of a beast who eats mostly plant-based foods, opportunistically supplemented by the occasional helping of animal tissue. Those textbook renderings of early hominids spearing mammoths and chasing herds over cliffs are biased portrayals. Early humans were gatherer-hunters (or perhaps more accurately: gatherer-scavengers), not the other way around.

If I could talk to that biologist today (sadly, he is now deceased), I would not quibble over teeth and spears. For me, the overarching medical argument for a plant-based diet is simply that we fare better on it than we do with the inclusion of meat. You could fill a bookshelf with studies demonstrating the benefits of vegan eating.

In my case, the decision to go veg was never a medical one. I did it for the animals. If there were no other reason than the suffering and untimely death of some 60 billion land animals a year (and comparable numbers of fishes) killed for human consumption each year, I would be as committed as a fastidious bunny-rabbit to shunning meat. On the flip side, the health, environmental and socio-economic benefits of vegetarianism are so compelling that even if meat without suffering was possible, I would remain a dedicated herbivore.

Today, aged 53 and feeling as fit and weighing slightly less than I did as a 22-year old collegiate swimmer, I thank Nada for showing me the joys of green foods, and animals everywhere for inspiring me not to eat their bodies.

Hamburger Helper
By Judy Carman, MA

Judy Carman is a long-time vegan, animal rights, environmental, peace and justice activist. She is the author of Peace to All Beings: Veggie Soup for the Chicken's Soul which was voted one of the best spiritual books of 2003 by Spirituality and Health magazine. She co-wrote with Tina Volpe The Missing Peace: The Hidden Power of our Kinship with Animals. Judy is co-founder of numerous activist groups, including the animal rights group Animal Outreach of Kansas. She is also co-founder (with Will and Madeleine Tuttle) of the Worldwide Prayer Circle for Animals at www.circleofcompassion.org and the Prayer Circle for Animals on Facebook. Her writing includes the "Eating as Though the earth Matters" column for Sierra Club's "Planet Kansas," a weekly article for prayer circle members, and her blog at www.peacetoallbeings.com where prayer flags for animals can be purchased.

A gravel road runs by our house. One morning during my walk along that road, I came upon a lovely snail who was trying to cross to the other side. The road is wide enough for two cars, and that's a long way for snails to crawl as the bits of gravel gradually gather on their sticky little bellies. So I picked her up (actually, no, I can't tell the difference between girl and boy snails, so I'm just guessing). Instead of retreating into her shell, she watched as I pulled the tiny pieces of grit from her tummy/foot. She seemed to look at me and then back at my hand cleaning her. There was a feeling that we were now friends and that gratitude was flowing back and forth between us. She—for being relieved of the gravel and being carried across the dangerous road, and me—for having the privilege of communing with this sacred little being. As Isaac Bashevis Singer wrote, "Even in the worm that crawls in the earth there glows a divine spark."

This is one of the many gifts and graces of living a nonviolent, vegan life. It is a feeling of wondrous connection with the living world that is set free once we no longer take part in violence against animals of the earth.

The story of how I went vegan is a bit like my snail friend's story of slowly crossing the road and accumulating lots of interfering bits and pieces along the way. It was a long process.

Although Donald Watson coined the term "vegan" in 1944, the year I was born, the news didn't reach me for quite some time. Raised in the '40's and '50's in the Midwest, the word "vegetarian" was either unknown or never uttered in my presence. We got our first television when I was about 9, but there was nothing about animal rights or veganism on Howdy Doody or Superman.

Our family had a deeper connection with meat eating and animal exploitation than most. My uncles ran the Kansas City stockyards, and Dad was a hunter of everything from tiny quails to giraffes and wolves. Our home décor included a polar bear rug upon which the dog would triumphantly pee, a zebra skin rug, and numerous severed heads of animals that once had families and freedom.

At home, animals were a strange mixture of the ones we loved (dogs, cats, and miscellaneous pets), the ones who were hunted with big guns, and those who were eaten. The in-betweens were the muskrats in the pond that Dad tried to shoot while I tried to bump his gun so he would miss; and the school rats I kept over the summer who multiplied from 3 to 30 in no time at all. Dad announced he was going to kill all of them, so I set them free, albeit to an unknown fate.

I was about 11 years old when our lambs disappeared, only to reappear on the dining room table. Like nearly all children, I felt a kinship with all animals, not just the dogs and cats. I had an innate sense that they were our friends. And like nearly all children, I didn't really grasp the fact that we were eating animals until that terrible meal of awakening. It never occurred to me that we would eat the lambs who only a few days before were nuzzling me and warming my heart.

Something stirred in me then, and I knew somehow I wanted to stop eating animals altogether. Unfortunately, my diet of chocolate covered doughnuts and Frosted Flakes did not do much for my health. It thrills me now to know that today's children, who feel as I did back then, can go online and discover how to pursue a healthy, vegan life, find like-minded friends, and honour the animals they love.

I ate very little meat after that awakening, but I had no idea that there were people who ate none, people who loved animals so much that they refused to eat them altogether, as well as refused to use them in other ways for entertainment, cleaning products, etc. Until—by grace—and much like my snail friend, I was lifted up. For me, that uplifting was information and like-minded souls.

In the '60's and '70's I was drawn to anti-nuke, environmental, and peace activism, as well as the emerging animal rights movement. This was pre-internet, but there were magazines, a growing number of books, including cookbooks and newly formed groups. We were questioning everything our culture had taught us. The worldview that animals and the earth were our property to do with as we wish was eroding dramatically for us.

Still, it took more snail time for me to fully comprehend the insanity of that worldview and to check off and eliminate, one by one, my own actions that were unconsciously based on that worldview. So I was vegetarian, not vegan, for many years. I was an extreme animal lover and wanted to dedicate my life to helping them, but it took undercover footage, animal rights books, and speakers, and intense conversations before the new worldview, the higher consciousness of true compassion, finally penetrated and transformed my mind. Animals are not ours to use, exploit, enslave or kill—this is surely one of the most radical and life-affirming revelations ever proposed to humanity—truly a spiritual, intellectual, moral, and ethical revolution.

The final breakthrough for me took place years ago with a simple phone call. I had been trying to ignore my inner wisdom that milk, cheese, and eggs reeked of cruelty. I was buying organic products to ease my unease. Finally, one day, I took a deep breath and called the organic Horizon Dairy. "What happens to the baby cows when they are born?" I asked. The calculated reply from the man on the other end of the line was: "We take them away from their mothers immediately so they won't bond." Being a mother myself and knowing that mothers bond with their babies long before birth and imagining the agony of that separation; my heart broke at such ignorance in the mind of one who is in control of so many precious lives. I continued, "So then when the mothers stop producing milk, what becomes of them?" One brutal word– "Hamburger," he said coldly. And that was it. Everything came into focus. I could see the whole picture of greed and power and how the animals need us all to stop this endless war against them. I am grateful to that man (my "hamburger" helper) for one thing—his cold and blunt reply was just the lift I needed to get completely across the road.

My spirit (just like the spirits of all people) has always known that animals were just as surely deserving of freedom and friendship as anyone in human form. My heart is at peace knowing I am being true to my spirit and demonstrating to others that, no matter how one is raised, we human beings can question everything we've been taught. We can dismiss, as

Walt Whitman said, "whatever insults your own soul", and as Martin Luther King said, "Never, never be afraid to do what's right, especially if the well-being of a person or animal is at stake. Society's punishments are small compared to the wounds we inflict on our soul when we look the other way."

We can synchronize our inner wisdom with our actions. We can live as joyful vegans and teach the world that every being on Earth is sacred and interconnected and that every being on Earth has the right to freedom and to celebrate life.

I am beyond grateful to all those who went before me researching, filming, rescuing, and educating to bring the horrors that people have perpetrated upon animals of the earth to light. May we all carry on that work and light the way for all children of every species; do all that we can to bring peace and liberation to the animal nations and lift up humanity to its highest calling to be "Homo Ahimsa"—the kind, compassionate, nonviolent species we were always meant to be.

Creative Maladjustment: From Civil Rights to Chicken Rights

By Karen Davis, PhD

Karen Davis, PhD is the President and Founder of United Poultry Concerns, a non-profit organization that promotes the compassionate and respectful treatment of domestic fowl, including a sanctuary for chickens on the Eastern Shore of Virginia. Her essays appear in *Experiencing Animal Minds* (2012), *Critical Theory and Animal Liberation* (2011), *Sister Species* (2011), *Animals and Women* (1995), and many other publications on the lives and feelings of animals and trans-species psychology. Her books include *Prisoned Chickens, Poisoned Eggs: An Inside Look at the Modern Poultry Industry*; *More Than a Meal: The Turkey in History, Myth, Ritual, and Reality*; *Instead of Chicken, Instead of Turkey: A Poultryless "Poultry" Potpourri*; *A Home for*

Henny; and *The Holocaust and the Henmaid's Tale: A Case for Comparing Atrocities*.

Karen and UPC are the subjects of the Genesis Award-winning article "For the Birds" in *The Washington Post*. In 2012, Karen was profiled in "Won't Back Down" in the *Altoona Mirror* in Pennsylvania where she grew up. In 2002, Karen Davis was inducted into the U.S. Animal Rights Hall of Fame "for outstanding contributions to animal liberation."

> "There are some things to which we must always be maladjusted if we are to be people of good will."
> **Martin Luther King Jr.**

As long as I can remember I've hated cruelty and helpless suffering. Growing up in a family and community where men and boys were expected to hunt, I watched my father and his friends pile their dogs into the trunks of their cars in the morning and return at the end of the day with the animals they had shot to be skinned and plucked in the cellar. As a teenager I started arguing with my father at the dinner table about hunting. We'd yell back and forth over prime rib or baked ham since it had not yet occurred to me that "meat" meant "animal" and murder.

In the mid-1950s, a teenage magazine ran a story called "Them!" "Them" referred to black students who were trying to enter the all-white high school in Little Rock, Arkansas, in a hate-filled atmosphere. I asked my father about the cause of this hate, which I could not understand. I don't recall his answer, but later when I was in college in the 1960s and starting to perceive the racial injustice there, he said if I ever brought a "coloured person" to our house, he would not let them in and coloured people didn't want to come to our house anyway.

When I challenged my father's attitude my mother said I should respect other people's opinions, but I replied I was only obliged to respect other people's right to *hold* an opinion, not the opinion itself.

Such moments marked the beginning of my conscious dissent from many conventional ways of thinking and acting. My sensibility began to take shape in the form of ideas and values that challenged prevailing sentiments. Learning what animals are forced to endure in order to become "meat," I became a vegetarian in 1974. Ten years later, after learning about the horrors of the dairy and egg industries, I became vegan.

During those years I agonized over the suffering and abuse of nonhuman animals. A trip to the Gulf of St. Lawrence where baby seal clubbing was going on, unbeknownst to me when I signed up for the tour, along with a visit to a large, dark warehouse in Maryland filled with thousands of parrots in tiny cages waiting to be sent to pet stores, awakened me deeply to the ubiquity of animal abuse and the hidden suffering of animals.

World Laboratory Animals Day in Lafayette Park in Washington, DC in 1983 was the turning point. As I looked at scenes of dogs and other animal victims from laboratories, the suffering in their eyes transfixed my attention. I pledged never again to abandon nonhuman animals to the inequity of our species because I couldn't bear the knowledge of their suffering. From that moment I became an animal rights activist, a creatively maladjusted person who seeks, works, and calls for a remedy.

In 1990, a crippled and abandoned chicken from the meat industry, named Viva, led me to found United Poultry Concerns, a non-profit organization dedicated to the compassionate and respectful treatment of chickens and other domestic fowl as well as a compassionate vegan diet and lifestyle.

When I met Viva in 1985, I was an English teacher at the University of Maryland expecting to teach English for the rest of my life. Yet I was devoting more and more time to animal issues, especially farmed animals. The number of these tortured beings was astonishing to me. Farmed animals were dismissed by environmentalists and others as 'beyond the pale' of moral concern because, they said, these animals were bred to a substandard state of intelligence and biological fitness and were "just food" that was "going to be killed anyway."

My experience with Viva showed otherwise. Though crippled, she was sensitive, affectionate, and alert. She already had a voice, including the sweetest trill when I gently stroked her feathers and talked to her softly, but her voice needed to be amplified within the oppressive system in which she and her sisters and brothers were trapped.

Working for chickens is an uphill climb, yet many people care deeply about chickens and the number who care is growing. Creative maladjustment means never adjusting to bigotry or nay saying. Instead, you keep faith with those you have chosen to fight for, and affirm what you know is right.

Compassion, Health and Nature – all Come Together

By Quinny Chiang

When I was asked to write my story, the first thought that came into my mind was that I have to tell it from the beginning. As a child, I spent an enormous amount of time with animals. Living in the city, surrounded by buildings and people, I found myself drawn to all living creatures. I often went to the aquariums nearby, the pet shops and zoos to look at animals without awareness that actually they were being treated as commodities. And, I too brought some home.

Growing up, I raised many small animals such as turtles, a rabbit, chicken and hamster, ducks and frogs. I was strongly connected and attached to all my companion animals. I would watch them eat, play with them and talk to them. They would respond and communicate. There was no doubt that I loved and respected them as individuals. Sadly, no matter how much I objected for some of my animals, they ended up on the dinner table. Unfortunately, even though I refused to eat them, I was having trouble seeing that farm animals were indeed the same as the animals that I played with.

I believe the urge to become vegetarian had stayed with me for many years. Although the motive was unclear, at some point in my 20's, I suddenly went on a vegetarian diet. Now that I think back, I could have been testing the waters. However, the real change did not happen back then. A year later, due to nutritional deficiency, I became very sick. I was ordered by my doctor to include meat in my diet. I didn't blame him because I was only eating leafy greens and rice at that time. After that incident, I did not think about vegetarianism for quite some time.

More than 10 years passed; one day, I met someone else who was on a vegetarian diet. We became friends and she invited me to the Vegetarian Food Fair. After I went to one of the lectures I was shocked. Not because I learned about the cruelty, but because I realized that I could no longer avoid the subject that I had avoided all this time. But the issue of cruelty gave me a legitimate reason to stop eating meat. I had finally awakened and switched to a vegetarian diet right away.

In reality though, I found it quite daunting to tell my friends and family about my switch. I spent the first few months transitioning to vegetarianism. Fortunately, I was accepted without too much fuss. And, believe me, the most troublesome part was that I kept feeling out-of-place when I was eating with others. But time helped. With a slow ease into the meatless diet, I even converted my husband to a vegetarian within a year.

Three years later, after going through many books and websites regarding animal rights issues, I decided it was time to go vegan. The transition to a vegan diet was fairly easy as I did not miss dairy products or eggs very much. It was the vegan lifestyle that took a bit of time, changing all my clothes was particularly difficult. I dislike wasting a perfectly wearable piece of clothing and I also dislike shopping for clothing unnecessarily. The way I resolved this issue was that I vowed to never buy a new piece of clothing that wasn't vegan. When the clothes are unusable, I will exchange them for something vegan. So that is coming along quite nicely.

Today, I'm so happy for the switch just from thinking of the animals I have saved. I feel so much more connected to animals and nature. Now that I come to think about it, this is the best thing that I have ever done.

My Visit to the Slaughterhouse
By Laura Lee

I moved to a farm when my mother remarried. There were cows there that would graze on grass in the fields. The cows were so large next to my tiny, eleven-year-old body, yet they were gentle giants whom I liked to pet and I looked forward to being around every day. One day, my step-father was heading out the door and asked if I wanted to go to the slaughterhouse with him. I said sure, even though I didn't know what it was; I just thought it was some kind of store.

We arrived at this large building. It smelled really bad from the outside and then when we walked in the smell got even worse. I had never smelled anything like that before. My step-father ushered me into a room and asked me to wait for him there while he went to pick up an order. In the room was a huge window. I looked through it and saw a floor covered with blood. I was confused, had someone gotten hurt? Should I find my dad to get help? I heard a squeal and looked up to see a pig had suddenly appeared in a metal barred type box, with walls two feet high. A man walked into the room wearing fishing boots and holding a rifle. He aimed the gun towards the frightened pig and shot him in the head. As soon as the pig fell down, dead, another pig was being forced out. The pig saw what happened to the other ahead of him; and, he was struggling, not wanting to go. He was so scared and I saw the fear in his eyes. Fear looks the same in an animal's eyes as it does in human eyes.

I was in shock; I couldn't believe what I had witnessed. I then realized where meat actually came from. Needless to say, my mother was very upset that my father had taken me to the slaughterhouse. He didn't see what the big deal was. His sons had all been there many times and never had a problem. As for me, I spent many days crying and not wanting to eat anything. I did not know that meat was not in everything. After all, my mother knew how much I loved animals, especially the ones on the farm, and she said nothing, year after year. I could not trust my mother anymore. It was just so hard for me to believe that other people knew that this was going on every day and were okay with it.

Thirty-eight years ago I was a naïve little 11-year-old girl who walked out of a slaughterhouse with the knowledge that changed how I would live the rest of my life. I've been a vegetarian since 1980 and a vegan since 2008. I would have been vegan from the start, but I was unaware of the cruelty involved in milk and egg products. I also know that they are not good for your health, but the cruelty aspect had always been my main concern.

A Journey from Denial to Compassionate Living
By Diane Gandee Sorbi

Diane Gandee Sorbi is an animal rights activist living in Redwood City, California, USA, with her vegan husband. She is an activist with Direct Action Everywhere, and enjoys reading, gardening, cooking delicious vegan food, and simple living. She doesn't watch television; she'd rather watch the world go vegan.

I was raised on the standard American diet and rarely questioned it. Before I even heard the word 'vegan' I would occasionally meet a person who was vegetarian. I was almost in awe of them. I realized they were living their values and making a compassionate choice, but I thought it would be too difficult to give up meat, so I would quickly push the thought out of my mind. But I knew that deep down, I wasn't proud of my choice to eat meat.

Several years ago, I began reading about the horrors of factory farming. I was heartbroken by what I learned and knew that if I didn't change, I wouldn't be able to live with myself. Unfortunately, around that time, I also started reading about so-called "humane" animal products. It seemed like the perfect solution. There would be no reason to give up anything. I could just pay more for things like grass-fed meat and cage-free eggs, and then animals wouldn't have to suffer. I told myself that those animals had long, happy lives, and if they were destined to become meat, they died a quick and painless death. I actually believed that dairy cows and laying hens lived out their natural life spans on small, bucolic farms and that nothing terrible could ever happen to them. I was incredibly naïve and chose to believe what I wanted to.

Shortly after joining Facebook I added a few new, vegan friends. At that point, I had no idea why anyone would choose to be vegan. I knew vegans didn't use or consume any animal products, but frankly, I thought they were a little strange. After all, what was the harm in taking eggs from chickens that naturally laid them or consuming milk from a cow or goat, since they needed to be milked? I never considered the fact that cows must first be pregnant in order to produce milk, and that their milk belonged only to their baby and that the baby would be chained in a tiny stall and made into veal. I was also clueless about the production of wool, which I assumed just involved giving the sheep a needed haircut.

Vegetarianism made sense, but veganism seemed extreme to me. I will always be grateful to those friends for opening my eyes. They posted articles and videos about the truth of dairy and eggs. From them, I learned that there was no such thing as humane animal products and that baby calves are torn from their grieving mothers only to produce veal and male baby chicks are ground up alive on the first day of birth because they are of no use to the industry. I was horrified! The blinders came off. There was no way to hide from the truth anymore.

I wish I had gone vegan immediately, but it took me a few months after I learned about vegetarianism. I started eliminating red meat, followed by poultry, fish, and eggs, getting used to living without them as I went along. My biggest stumbling block, and what took the longest, was cheese. It was my favourite food and I ate a lot of it. There was another reason I didn't go vegan right away: I was worried about social gatherings. I didn't want to attend gatherings where food was served and be that weird vegan munching on celery sticks while everyone else was eating the rest of the food. Also, I sometimes enjoyed eating in restaurants and figured there would be nothing I could order but salad. I knew these were purely selfish reasons, and my conscience was never at peace; I could no longer enjoy my meals because I realized how much suffering they were causing. I knew the time had come to take the leap.

The day I committed to becoming vegan was one of the best and most meaningful days of my life. It felt as if I were skydiving out of a plane for the first time; it would feel scary, but exhilarating. There was no turning back. My first, delicious, vegan meal was a revelation. When you know that no innocent beings were intentionally harmed or killed for you, it feels amazing!

Although I went vegan initially for animals, I have experienced many more benefits after becoming vegan. My health has improved exponentially. Many chronic ailments, from asthma to skin problems, have vanished. My cholesterol levels and blood pressure, once very high, are now excellent. I'd struggled for many years to lose about 40 excess pounds, but in vain. The weight came off, effortlessly, less than a year after becoming vegan. I have tons more energy than ever before. I can honestly say that I feel at least 20 years younger.

As someone who cares about social justice issues and the environment, I'm glad to know that my diet is a solution to world hunger and helps with problems like global warming. Realizing that I had the power to change the world for the better through veganism, I've become involved in activism, which is very fulfilling. I've had the pleasure of meeting many wonderful people in the vegan community. I think of them as my family. I absolutely love being vegan! My only regret is that I didn't do it earlier.

How I Became Vegan
By David Sztybel, PhD

David Sztybel is an animal rights philosopher. His Ph.D. from the University of Toronto is in animal ethics, and he also completed a post-doctoral fellowship at Queen's University. He has taught many animal rights courses at Brock University, has had several peer-reviewed journal and encyclopedia articles, and maintains his website at www.davidsztybel.info, which also links to his blog. He has been a vegan since 1988.

What inspired me to go vegan? As is the case with many people, especially from around that generation, I was inspired by one particular book, Animal Liberation by Peter Singer.

I used to haunt the World's Biggest Bookstore in downtown Toronto. One day, I was unaccountably drawn to Singer's book and decided to read it. I took in his lucid reasoning (although now I take issue with a number of his ideas), and his detailing of factory farming and vivisection. I stumbled out of my bedroom and said to my mother something like, "The way they treat these animals in factory farming is so horrible…" She interrupted me and finished my sentence: "So you want to be a vegetarian? Okay." From then on she cooked such meals. My sister Miriam was already a vegetarian for many years, although she never breathed a word about it to me. My mother and father went vegetarian years later, and she said she was being vegetarian vicariously through her children prior to that time. The death of the family dog brought on my mother's conversion, and she eventually persuaded my father to follow suit.

Since I left the nest I have learned vegan cooking and offer a modest cookbook on my website with some of my family's favourite recipes. The truth is that I had not yet decided to be a vegetarian, but my mother finished my thought, and for the life of me I could not think of a more appropriate conclusion. This conversion to veganism shaped my career as a philosophy student and scholar.

The best reason to go vegan is for animals, but the environmental and health reasons only make conditions better for all animals too, if only indirectly. There is an incredible array of reasons for going vegan, and only pitifully few excuses for omnivorism that give up the ghost on close examination. I hope that people will energize such life-giving transformation on an ever-broader scale.

My Vegan Experience
By Coleen Tew

I had always felt a kinship with animals, especially in my teenage years when I railed against the hunting of whales, harp seals, and other wildlife. It never occurred to me that animals we called food were sentient; in fact, my religion (Catholic) taught us that animals have no souls, ergo, feel no pain. Even my own father told me that cows and pigs were so dull that they barely even knew they existed. This, of course, helped me to eat them with impunity. I tried to be vegetarian several times during my twenties and thirties, but gave in to peer pressure when others called me a kook and an inconvenience.

It wasn't until June of 2005 that something really switched in my head and heart. I had sat down to eat a chicken breast for dinner, just as I had many times in the past. But, when I cut into it, I saw with great clarity the grain of the breast meat and knew beyond a shadow of a doubt that I could never again eat meat. All I could think of at that moment was that this "meat" had once been a living being and that it had died for my dinner. That thought repulsed me, and I was overwhelmed with guilt and shame that it had taken me so long to figure this out.

Some time later, I thought I should check out the PETA website to find other sources of protein (I was still convinced that protein was the foundation of good health). I clicked on "Meet your Meat", expecting a light-hearted romp through meadows with animals. The few seconds I had the courage to watch, and listen to, are burned forever into my memory. My heart was pounding, and I was sobbing with grief. After I had calmed down, I listened to a speech given by Ingrid Newkirk about veganism, and the cruelty involved in the production of dairy and eggs. I was thinking to myself, how are these foods cruel? Animals don't die...do they? As I read further and watched (or tried to watch) the videos of the terrible abuse in the dairy and egg industries, I knew that night I had become a vegan.

I thought it would be difficult, given my propensity toward conformity, to be one who eats differently and speaks out against the abuse of animals. Surprisingly, it came quite naturally. Yes, I do feel alienated at times, but I always keep in mind images of factory farms and slaughterhouses; nothing could equal that pain, and I will never stop advocating for them.

I am happier, healthier and, without the burden of guilt, lighter in spirit; my taste buds are more refined, and I enjoy food so much more than I ever have. Going vegan was absolutely the best decision I have ever made, and I hope more people wake up and embrace compassion.

How I Went Vegan
By Matt Bear

Matt Bear grew up in Minnesota on his grandparents' animal farm. Through his teens, he lived and worked on an intensive pig factory farm. Matt is a popular speaker and teacher, drawing on his first-hand experience with farmed animals, his dedication to social justice issues, and his broad understanding of the impact our consumer choices have on those with whom we share the world.

Matt founded NonviolenceUnited.org, created the popular VEGAN shirt from VeganShirt.com, and produced the widely acclaimed video A Life Connected (VeganVideo.org) – now available in sixteen languages and seen by millions around the world. Matt currently serves as Director of Vegan

Projects at Farm Animal Rights Movement (FARM) and continues to direct Nonviolence United.

I cherish the years I spent on my grandparents' farm. I remember waking up to roosters crowing and the clank of the covers on metal feeding troughs slapping closed as pigs finished eating and turned to lie in the morning sun. I can still smell the magic of Grandma's breakfast drifting upstairs to pull me out of bed.

I'd jump into my overalls and scramble out to help Grandpa feed the forty sheep, two steers, and the fifty or so pigs. The farm had changed over the years. The gigantic red barn that had once housed dozens of dairy cows was now nearly empty. It echoed with the calls of the remaining few sheep and low of the steers. Grandma collected the eggs from the fifty or sixty chickens and washed them -- ready for her famous cakes and cookies, and for neighbours to buy a few dozen at a time.

In the spring, Grandpa would come home from the feed store with dozens of little yellow chicks, only a few days old, peeping and blinking at their new world. Grandma would set up the brooder house where the chicks would spend their lives over the next few months. They would peck and scratch the ground outside during the day, and at night they would huddle under heat lamps, locked up safe from the night.

When I was seven years old, I quickly became friends with one particular chick. He wasn't any smaller or bigger than the others, but we had a connection. When I would walk in to sit and watch the baby chickens while the others would nervously scatter to the other side of the small shed, he would come running to me. He'd jump in my lap to be held and petted. He had a way of looking me in the eye. He seemed like a long-lost friend somehow trapped in the world of being a chicken. I named him Foghorn. And I loved him.

Chickens grow fast. Soon August arrived. My aunts, uncles, and cousins rolled down the dusty gravel road toward the farm to take part in the traditional family event. Grandma boiled water in huge pots out in the pump house and Grandpa sharpened the long, steel blade of a homemade machete.

Midmorning came. My cousins picked up the nearly full-grown chickens by their legs and carried them to Grandpa. I followed behind, cradling Foghorn. I handed Foghorn to Grandpa. Foghorn looked at me and blinked. With one giant hand, Grandpa folded Foghorn's wings to his sides, held his legs and laid him down on the tree stump. Seconds later, he handed Foghorn's bleeding body back to me. I held him upside down by his legs as I was told to do and let the blood drain from his severed neck. As I stood in line with my cousins to take Foghorn to the scalding pots to make it easier to pluck out his feathers, I looked back at his head lying in a heap with the others… one last blink, beak open.

I was lost in a fog of confusion. I was proud of the tradition and proud of helping the grownups. But a friendship was lost that day, along with my kindred spirit. And a trust was broken – trust between my grandparents and myself, and trust between me and my chicken friend. While my remembrance speech at the dinner table that night kept everyone from eating the chicken, it didn't stop them – or me – for long. I was told, and I was convinced, "It is just a part of life."

I spent my teen years living and working on a pig factory farm. My mother had married my step-father who owned what used to be a farm, but was quickly turning into a facility. My stepbrothers and I ran the daily operations – I had my hands in every gory detail. I had nightmares from what I saw and what I did still keeps me up nights – even after all these years. Immersed in the horror, I continued to tell myself, "It is just a part of life."

I was eighteen and in college when I heard the word "vegetarian" for the first time. While on a field trip, where I met my wife Barbara, one of our professors ordered pizza without pepperoni. I thought he had to be crazy. I'd steal glances at him eating a peanut butter and jelly sandwich while others stuffed their hands into a zip lock bag of beef jerky. I learned that he was vegetarian for environmental reasons. At the time, the reasons didn't matter to me as much as the sudden realization that there was another way – keeping and killing animals was not "just a part of life." That was a lie. It was all a lie.

When Barbara came with me from college for a visit to the "farm," I suddenly saw everything differently. A sick mother pig opened my eyes and changed my life forever. I'd seen downed mother pigs dozens of times before. Female pigs are impregnated over and over again. They get so used up over their short lives that their health often deteriorates – often so badly that they lie down and simply can't get up again. Anyone who thinks this doesn't happen because "farmers care for their animals because they care, or because they are the farmers' livelihood," just doesn't understand the enormity of these facilities, the pressures of modern day farming, and the realities of using animals for profit. It is less expensive to push a used up sow aside than to care for her. And that's what animal farms are all about – making money.

I looked into that momma pig's eyes and it felt like a movie moment – she entered my heart. I gave her a little food and water – she couldn't reach it by herself. I still have a hard time thinking about this as I write about it over twenty years later. I told my step-father about her. He handed me a gun, but I just couldn't take her life. I couldn't bring myself to put her out of her misery. Barbara and I gave her a little more water and food, got back in the car, and cried on our way back to school. We talked about her all the way. We talked about the family farm, about the whole animal agribusiness industry, about the waste and violence. We talked about how it was all so unnecessary. We made a commitment to each other and a promise to that momma pig – we'd go vegetarian. I have never gone back to that farm again.

It took us a few years to go fully vegetarian. At the time, we lived in a very rural community, in a tiny house directly across the street from a Hardee's hamburger joint and a Dairy Queen. We could just about read the giant, behind-the-counter menus from our living room. We knew only two vegetarians and wouldn't hear the word "vegan" for another three years. But we persevered and moved along the path – refusing to buy flesh, but still eating it with family and friends.

That's the power of culture – we knew it was wrong, it went against our own values, but still we struggled to live our own values.

Then, on New Year's Eve 1989, after we'd both graduated college and moved out of state, we pulled a packet of steaks from the freezer. The steaks had been a Christmas gift from a family member. We cooked up the steaks, but couldn't eat them. We looked at each other… and we looked at those steaks. "Let's not do this anymore." The promise stuck. We had gone vegetarian.

Shortly thereafter we were gleefully shopping in our local co-op for rennet-free cheese and free range eggs, patting ourselves on the back for our thoughtful choices, when a new friend of ours, who happened to be vegan offered, "If you're vegetarian for animals, you should look into going vegan." What the heck is "vay-gun?" we thought. Her comment set us on the vegan path and onto what has become our life's work.

This all happened before the Internet. The only dairy-free milk on the shelf was gritty soy milk that I had to plug my nose to get down. Our first experiment with homemade seitan kept seitan off my radar for years because I thought it was supposed to be a blobby mess. There were no commercially available vegan cheeses or ice creams (that we could find). I feel like going vegan twenty years ago took quite a bit of willpower and diligence. And maybe it still does today, but times have changed. Now, even the most modest supermarkets in the Midwest where I grew up have vegan ice creams, cheeses, milks, hotdogs, burgers and so much more. Going vegan is easier than ever.

Now, nearly everyone I meet knows what "vegan" means. More and more people understand why choosing vegan is such an important and powerful consumer choice. Because of this shift, the way I do outreach leafleting has shifted too. My days of debating, arguing, and trying to convince people to consider vegan food are quickly becoming days destined to teach the eager about the vegan path.

Today, the old family farm is empty. Grandma died recently and the homestead will likely soon be sold. She'd kept the big barn painted and in repair, fulfilling a promise to my Grandpa who passed away in 1988. Grandpa saw, even then, that the family farm had become a thing of the past. The surrounding farmsteads now stand empty, barns crumbling to the ground. The few that survived have become intensive factory farms where animals spend their lives in misery and confinement.

Factory farms are so hellish that people have come to revere smaller, family farms because they badly want a release from the pain, from the horror. "We can't do that to animals, can we?" they tell themselves. "Of course not – look at all the "humane" farms." And it all feels better... for a little while. But it is just another lie. We lie to ourselves that animals we are using and eating must somehow have magically missed the mutilations, the broken families, the confinement, the life at the total mercy of humans, and the final, ultimate cruelty of stealing their precious lives from them.

Of course, there is no such thing as "humane" animal farming. I've lived it; I know. Even on the smallest, most thoughtful of family farms, like my grandparents' farm, the animals will be used against their will and die before their time. Yes, there may be opportunities to be "less cruel", but not "humane." It is another lie.

Labeling animal products as "humane" is a marketing ploy to bilk good people who honestly want to do the right thing. People who, like me, don't realize that there is a better, nonviolent way; people who don't realize that eating animals is not "just a part of life." We want to escape the pain, the horror, and I understand that. I want to escape it, too, but animals can never escape it. Happily, there is a solution.

Vegan choices offer a powerful opportunity to stop the suffering and death inflicted on others. Vegan choices offer each of us an escape from the pain of being part of this cycle of misery. Our freedom and our redemption lies in no longer taking part in the suffering of others. Choosing vegan is when I became free, it is when I became happy, it is when I fully became the person I think I always was but hadn't met yet – someone who passionately and unapologetically cares.

AFTERWORD

It has been such a blessing being able to tell my story. For five years, sitting hour after hour in front of my computer, sometimes with my eyes turning red because I was not able to sleep, I kept typing and typing. Even now, as I write this, many thoughts spring to mind that I want to write, but I keep telling myself that the message needs to be brought out. Otherwise, I could be writing this forever, adding more and more pages.

No longer is veganism a secret, a cult, or something extreme or radical. No longer are we hippies that only eat carrots and beans. We are the ones who really care about everyone and want to get the message out to the masses.

This book came to be in August of 2010 when I said, "You know I need to tell my story to the world. My awakening inspires everyone."

It is sad that now, as I write this, millions upon millions of non-human animals are being butchered alive and millions upon millions of humans are starving just so we can eat the ones we butcher. You see how perverse this is?

But there is good news. No longer do we have to support these atrocities. We can be the minority that joins the compassionate ones and lives a good and righteous life. Every day thousands are joining and celebrating and loving life. Although the change is not as fast as I wish it was, nonetheless we are making progress.

Some thirty years ago, who ever thought of going to the supermarket to find vegan coconut ice cream or vegan ribs and chicken? There are literally thousands of options, comfort and health foods alike, organic produce is hitting the supermarket shelves every day. More people are demanding wholesome foods. Once ten percent of the world's population declares they are vegan, there will be a domino effect; every fast food chain, every supermarket, and every restaurant will have vegan items. And it is now happening. As of 2011, the

Loving Hut chain of vegan restaurants is now the fastest growing vegan restaurant in the world, with more than 200 locations worldwide since April 2008.[1]

The solution is simple. Go vegan or we will all perish. But it is not as simple as that. Of course, I could have told everyone simply to go vegan because it is better for their health, for the planet and animals. But what will that do when everyone is so ingrained in a culture that sees animals merely as property? Even though it is true, it is that simple, I had to find a way to explain it to people. I had so many ideas that I actually had to rewrite this book and edit it many times. I thought it was not good enough. That is why it has taken longer to write than I expected.

Hopefully, one day, this book will become an international bestseller. And though I always like to think big, I will be glad if just a thousand people read this work and are inspired to become vegan activists and change the world. I do not mind if a million people read it, of course, that would be even better.

I never dreamt that one day I would be writing a book; English was one of my worst subjects in school. Actually, I hated school, I just wanted to get out as fast as I could and have fun. But what fun? I did not have many friends or aspirations in life. I surely did not know what I wanted out of life. I did the odd job here and there, working on assembly lines, in warehouses and factories, in general labourer-type jobs.

It has been such a pleasure writing this book, and from the bottom of my heart I thank everyone who has helped me on this journey and those of you who are reading this. Without you this book would not have made it this far.

After 10,000 years of domination, we can now look at animals in the eye and beg for their forgiveness. Are they meant to live in tiny wire cages, or on top of one another? Are they meant to be at our mercy? As I sit here writing this, millions upon millions of them are confined to pens or cages and the rest of them are waiting to be slaughtered. It is sad that I am not able to save all of them or that people are not waking up fast enough. It is sad that we have stooped so low in our evolution. How did we manage to become so sadistic?

It is my hope for all of us to live in a world at peace, in an Eden-like paradise. No longer can we ignore the simple fact that veganism is indeed the solution to all our problems. I have been so blessed to be given this gift from the Universe to tell my story. My vision is to spread this book, as far and as wide and to as many people as possible. And only you can take the next evolutionary step toward peace and freedom.

Thank you very much for reading this book. Please pass it on to as many people as you can.

For further updates on my work visit my website at:
www.michaellanfield.com

For the official site for the book and film visit:
www.weareinterconnected.com

Visit the online vegan community, The Vegan Sandwich
http://thevegansandwich.com

REFERENCES

Chapter One – How Life Started: The Herding Culture

1. Tuttle, Will. Chapter 2, Our Culture's Roots, The World Peace Diet: Eating for Spiritual Health and Social Harmony. Lantern Books, 2005. Print, Page 18.
2. Herding. National Geographic Education. National Geographic Society. http://bit.ly/1FYkOtI
3. Hamilton, Richard. Agriculture's Sustainable Future: Breeding Better Crops. Scientific American. http://bit.ly/1FYljUq
4. Rensberger, Boyce. Teeth Show Fruit Was The Staple: No Exceptions Found. New York Times. May 15, 1979. Section Science Time, Page C1.
5. Greger, Michael. Calculate Your Healthy Eating Score. NutritionFacts.org Vol. 5, August 24, 2011. http://bit.ly/1G9T7U6
6. Wilford, John Noble. Some Prehumans Feasted on Bark Instead of Grasses. The New York Times, June 27, 2012. http://nyti.ms/1aILk1t
7. Human as Frugivore. http://bit.ly/1J06s1U
8. 22nd World Vegetarian Congress 1973, Ronneby Brunn, Sweden.
9. McClellan, James Edward; Dorn, Harold. Science and technology in world history: an introduction. Johns Hopkins University Press. Print. Page 11. http://bit.ly/1JkfLq9
10. Hunting: The Murderous Business - Anti-Hunting - In Defense of Animals. http://bit.ly/1DTsfE4
11. Mahon KL, Escott-Stump. Krause's Food, Nutrition, and Diet Therapy. 9th edition W.B. Saunders Co., 1996.
12. Mills, Milton. The Comparative Anatomy of Eating. http://bit.ly/1byDGrE
13. Greger, Michael. Infectious Diseases, Climate Change, Influenza. https://youtu.be/G20cooZOiYE
14. MacKenzie D. Genes of deadly bird flu reveal Chinese origin. New Scientist, 2006. http://bit.ly/1Fh3tjF
15. Greger, Michael. Extreme Remedies are the most appropriate for extreme diseases, Bird Flu Book Online http://bit.ly/1Jy5WoP
16. Greger, Michael. Bird Flu: A Virus of Our Own Hatching. Lantern, 2006. Print. Page 346.
17. Greens/EFA in the European Parliament. 2004. Avian influenza and the globalized food trade: EU must act to halt global food diseases. News release, January 27.
18. Greger, Michael. Infectious Diseases, Climate Change, Influenza. https://youtu.be/G20cooZOiYE
19. Ibid.

Chapter Two – Environmental Destruction

1. Hamilton, Tracey. Pythagoras' Views on Female, Animal, and Plant Rights: The Path to Ecocentrism and Enlightenment. Professor Kenneth Dorter, Print.
2. International Panel for Sustainable Resource Management, Assessing the Environmental Impacts of Consumption and Production, United Nations Environment Programme 2010. http://bit.ly/1K9ympY
3. Steinfeld, H., Gerber P., Wassenaar, T., Castel, V., Rosales, M. & Haan, C., Livestock's Long Shadow: Environmental Issues and Options, Rome, Food and Agriculture Organization of the United Nations, xxi. 2006.
4. Goodland, Robert, and Jeff Anhang. Livestock and Climate Change. World Watch Institute, Page 11. Print., November/December 2009
5. Ching Hai, Supreme Master. From Crisis to Peace - The Organic Vegan Way Is the Answer. The Supreme Master Ching Hai Association, 2010, 2011. www.crisis2peace.org
6. Eighty Percent of Global Warming Would Stop If World Goes Veg. SOS Global Warming. Supreme Master Television, July 3, 2008. http://bit.ly/1JyecVU
7. Bell, Dan. The Methane Makers. BBC News. October 28, 2009. http://bbc.in/1IN4mzq
8. A Delicate Balance - The Truth. Aaron Scheibner. Phoenix Philms, 2008. DVD. www.adelicatebalance.com.au
9. Reducing Shorter-Lived Climate Forcers through Dietary Change. World Preservation Foundation, Page 8. http://bit.ly/1FhaBfS
10. Hertwich, E., van der Voet, E., Suh, S., Tukker, A, Huijbregts M., Kazmierczyk, P., Lenzen, M., McNeely, J., Moriguchi, Y., UNEP Assessing the Environmental Impacts of Consumption and Production: Priority Products and Materials, A Report of the Working Group on the Environmental Impacts of Products and Materials to the International Panel for Sustainable Resource Management. Page 82.
11. A Life Connected: Vegan. Bear, Matt. Nonviolenceunited.org http://veganvideo.org
12. Wodzak, Mango. Eden Fruitarianism: Environmental Issues Destination Eden. Lulu Press Inc., 2013. 122. Print.
13. Thirsty Food: Fuelling Agriculture to Fuel Humans. National Geographic. http://on.natgeo.com/1QoSzwm
14. Global Meat Production and Consumption Continue to Rise. Worldwatch Institute, October 11, 2011. http://bit.ly/1JkfLq9
15. How Much Water to Make a Pound of Beef? How Much Water to Make a Pound of Beef? Vegsource.com, March 1, 2001. http://bit.ly/1I0tNiI
16. Goodland, Robert, and Jeff Anhang. Livestock and Climate Change. Worldwatch Insitute, November-December 2009. http://bit.ly/1byPBpA

17. Food and Agriculture Organization of the United Nations. Livestock's Long Shadow – Environmental Issues and Options. Rome. 2006. http://bit.ly/1HsDOWT
18. How Fruits Will Save the World: The Sweet, Simple Solution. FoodNSport, December 28, 2012. https://youtu.be/oLKKVBCE2nI
19. Food and Agriculture Organization of the United Nations. Livestock's Long Shadow – Environmental Issues and Options. Rome. 2006. http://bit.ly/1HsDOWT

Chapter Three – Health Implications

1. Greger, Michael. Lose Weight Without Losing Your Health —or Your Life. Atkins Exposed. 6th Edition Volume 2. Page 35. Reprinted from Dr. Greger's free monthly newsletter: Latest in Human Nutrition, June 2004.
2. Wodzak, Mango. Destination Eden. Lulu, 2013. Print. http://amzn.to/1OipGnb
3. CBAN - Canadian Biotechnology Action Network. GE Crops and Foods (On the Market) / Topics / Resources / Take Action. CBAN (The Canadian Biotechnology Action Network). http://bit.ly/1FhT8DU
4. Labeling. Labeling / Topics / Resources / Take Action. CBAN - Canadian Biotechnology Action Network, http://bit.ly/1Pq9ahV
5. Campbell, T. Colin, and Thomas M. Campbell. Lessons From China. The China Study: The Most Comprehensive Study of Nutrition Ever Conducted and the Startling Implications for Diet, Weight Loss and Long-term Health. Dallas, TX: BenBella, 2005. 79. Print.
6. Scheibner, Aaron. Cancer Grows in Three Stages. A Delicate Balance - The Truth. Phoenix Philms, 2008. PDF. Page 36.
7. Foods: Powerful for Health. PCRM (Physicians Committee for Responsible Medicine). http://bit.ly/1Gn7th2
8. Barnard, Neal, and Jennifer Raymond. Chapter 10: Cancer Pain. Foods That Fight Pain: Revolutionary New Strategies for Maximum Pain Relief. Harmony, 1998. Print Page 291.
9. Ibid. Page 78.
10. Freeman, Mason W., and Christine Junge. The Harvard Medical School Guide to Lowering Your Cholesterol. McGraw-Hill, 2005. Print.
11. Greger, Michael, MD. Mitochondrial Theory of Aging. NutritionFacts.org, December 28, 2010. http://bit.ly/1INQPro
12. 40 Year Vegan Dies of a Heart Attack! Why? The Omega-3 and B12 Myth with Dr. Michael Greger. 2003. http://youtu.be/q7KeRwdIH04
13. Campbell, T. Colin, and Thomas M. Campbell. Lessons From China. The China Study: The Most Comprehensive Study of Nutrition Ever Conducted and the Startling Implications for Diet, Weight Loss and Long-term Health. BenBella, 2005. Print. Page 80.
14. Graham, Douglas, Chapter 6. Protein: 10% Maximum. The 80/10/10 Diet: Balancing Your Weight, and Life One Luscious Bite at a Time. Key Largo: FoodnSport, 2006. Print Page 104.

15. Freedman, Rory, and Kim Barnouin. Chapter 7: The Myths and Lies About Protein. Skinny Bitch: A No-nonsense, Tough-love Guide for Savvy Girls Who Want to Stop Eating Crap and Start Looking Fabulous! Running, 2005. Print. Page 85.
16. Barnard, Neal, and Jennifer Raymond. Chapter 1: Oh, my Aching Back! Foods That Fight Pain: Revolutionary New Strategies for Maximum Pain Relief. Harmony, 1998. Print. Page 48.
17. Graham, Douglas, Chapter 6. Protein: 10% Maximum. The 80/10/10 Diet: Balancing Your Weight, and Life One Luscious Bite at a Time. Key Largo: FoodnSport, 2006. Print. Pages 99 - 102.
18. Campbell, T. Colin, T. Colin Campbell Promoting The 80/10/10 Diet. https://youtu.be/l9F_2aQnSnI
19. Protein and Amino Acid Requirements in Human Nutrition. WHO/FAO/UNU Expert Consultation, 2002, 2007. http://bit.ly/1yYg9uT
20. Graham, Douglas N. Chapter 6. Protein: 10% Maximum. The 80/10/10 Diet: Balancing Your Weight, and Life One Luscious Bite at a Time. Key Largo: FoodnSport, 2006. Print. Page 108.
21. Gale Jack, Osteoporosis: The Silent Threat, Macrobiotics Today. March/April 1992, Vol. 32, No. 2
22. The Protein Myth with Running Raw Project: Tim Van Orden. March 19, 2008. https://youtu.be/ae-dlHOmwk4
23. Scheibner, Aaron. Protein. A Delicate Balance - The Truth. Phoenix Philms, 2008. PDF. Page 33.
24. Ibid. Page 19.
25. Graham, Douglas, Chapter 7. Fat: 10% Maximum. The 80/10/10 Diet: Balancing Your Weight, and Life One Luscious Bite at a Time. Key Largo: FoodnSport, 2006. Print. Pages 110-112.
26. Ibid. Page 114.
27. Prenatal Nutrition Guidelines for Health Professionals - Fish and Omega-3 Fatty Acids. Health Canada, April 28, 2009. http://bit.ly/1yYkLB4
28. Tuttle, Will. Chapter Six: Hunting and Herding Sea Life. The World Peace Diet: Eating for Spiritual Health and Social Harmony. Lantern, 2005. Print. Page 96.
29. Scheibner, Aaron. Fish. A Delicate Balance - The Truth. Phoenix Philms, 2008. 98. Print.
30. Ibid. Page 99.
31. Plant Sources of Omega 3s. Cleveland Clinic. http://cle.clinic/1aWc2DR
32. Scheibner, Aaron. A Delicate Balance - The Truth. Phoenix Philms, 2008. 21 min. Film.
33. Barnard, Neal, and Joanne Stepaniak. Breaking the Food Seduction: The Hidden Reasons behind Food Cravings-- and 7 Steps to End Them Naturally. St. Martin's, 2003. Print. Page 53.

34. Freedman, Rory, and Kim Barnouin. Chapter 11. Skinny Bastard: A Kick-in-the-ass for Real Men Who Want to Stop Being Fat and Start Getting Buff. Running, 2009. Print.
35. Michael Greger, How Much Pus is there in Milk? NutritionFacts.org, September 8, 2011. http://bit.ly/1yYqZAQ
36. 150 times more contaminated with blood, pus and feces. Natural News. http://bit.ly/1JC0t0o
37. Barnard, Neal D., and Joanne Stepaniak. Breaking the Food Seduction: The Hidden Reasons behind Food Cravings and 7 Steps to End Them Naturally. St. Martin's, 2003. Print. Page 54.
38. Cronometer.com, https://cronometer.com
39. Addicted to Cheese and Ice Cream? The Opiate Qualities of Dairy. Free From Harm. http://bit.ly/1PC4aoH
40. Campbell, T. Colin, and Thomas M. Campbell. Turning off Cancer. The China Study: The Most Comprehensive Study of Nutrition Ever Conducted and the Startling Implications for Diet, Weight Loss and Long-term Health. BenBella, 2005. Print. Page 59.
41. Cronometer.com, https://cronometer.com
42. Greger, Michael. Is One Egg a Day Too Much? August 26, 2008. NutritionFacts.org http://bit.ly/1JimqEM
43. Health Risks and Dangers of Eating Eggs, Dherbs.com http://bit.ly/1QpJyDs
44. Scheibner, Aaron. Protein Content of Various Foods. A Delicate Balance - The Truth. Phoenix Philms, 2008. PDF. Pages 73-74.
45. Mangels, Reed. Calcium in the Vegan Diet. From Simply Vegan, 5th Edition. The Vegetarian Resource Group, http://bit.ly/1GnRlyS
46. Mangels, Reed. Iron in the Vegan Diet. From Simply Vegan, 5th Edition. The Vegetarian Resource Group, http://bit.ly/1QpQ0dA
47. Veganism in a Nutshell – Vegan Nutrition. The Vegetarian Resource Group. http://bit.ly/1Pr7LrA
48. Greger, Michael. Preventing the Most Common Diseases, Dr. Michael Greger, 2013. https://youtu.be/5bcdCPOXm8o
49. Vegan Starter Kit. IDA / Mercy for Animals. 2007. Page 2. http://bit.ly/1Ekc2t8

Chapter Four – Animal Agriculture

1. Quote by Issaac Bashevis Singer. goodreads. http://bit.ly/1HxSKkW
2. Ching Hai, Supreme Master. Chapter 3: Gove Life to Save Life. From Crises to Peace: The Organic Vegan Way is the Answer. Online. http://bit.ly/1I1vsVa
3. Facts and Figured, PhilipLymbery.com. http://bit.ly/1QpWiKl
4. Farm Animals. Animal Alliance of Canada. http://bit.ly/1EwLff5
5. FARM - Benefits of Vegan. Farm Animal Rights Movement (FARM). http://bit.ly/1Go4hEG
6. Don't Buy the Myth. Humanemyth.org. http://bit.ly/1JixXUz
7. Fowl Play Movie: A Documentary about the Egg Industry. Mercy for Animals, 2008. http://fowlplaymovie.com

8. Welfare Issues for Egg laying Hens, Compassion in World Farming. http://bit.ly/1DVRx4z
9. Lin, Doris. What Is Forced Molting? About.com Animal Rights. http://abt.cm/1Dplszu
10. Farm to Fridge. Mercy for Animals. February 3, 2011. https://youtu.be/ju7-n7wygP0
11. Ibid.
12. Broilers, Wikipedia. http://bit.ly/1bzoz15
13. Life Span of a Pet Chicken, Backyard Chickens. http://bit.ly/1PrStTw
14. Turkeys - Woodstock Farm Animal Sanctuary. http://bit.ly/1zSKaqH
15. Broilers, Wikipedia. http://bit.ly/1bzoz15
16. 5 Incredibly Intelligent Animals. Readers Digest Canada. http://bit.ly/1DpE1Ue
17. Perry, Joellen and Jacoby, Mary. These Little Pigs Get Special Care From Norwegians, The Wall Street Journal, August 6, 2007.
18. Chapter 4: The Pig - Unit 33: Castrating the Piglet. Food and Agriculture Organization of the United Nations. http://bit.ly/1zSVOSu
19. Earthlings. By Shaun Monson. Narration Joaquin Phoenix. Music, Moby. 2005. DVD.
20. Ibid.
21. Ibid.
22. Farm Animals and Us. CIWF. https://youtu.be/RpzpUeJ9HA8
23. How to Artificially Inseminate Cows and Heifers. WikiHow. http://bit.ly/1JAbKOJ
24. Simultaneous Lactation and Pregnancy. Viva! http://bit.ly/1Go9bin
25. Lyman, Howard and Merzer, Glen. Mad Cowboy: Plain Truth from the Cattle Rancher Who Won't Eat Meat. Scribner, 1998. http://amzn.to/1aWW10g
26. Cow's Milk and the Problems with It, Beautiful Vegan. http://bit.ly/1HyyEXI
27. Dairy: Slaughter and Disease, Liberation BC. http://bit.ly/1JAegV2
28. Peaceable Kingdom: The Journey Home. Director Jenny Stein. Producer James La Veck. Performer Harold Brown, Howard Lyman, Cayce Mell, Cheri Ezell-Vandersluis, Willow Jeane Lyman, Jim Vandersluis and Jason Tracy. Tribe of Heart, 2009. DVD.
29. Earthlings. By Shaun Monson. Narration, Joaquin Phoenix. Music, Moby. 2005. DVD. 21:20 min.
30. Food: Is Veal Cruel? BBC http://bit.ly/1GocZjI
31. Peaceable Kingdom: The Journey Home. Director Jenny Stein. Producer James La Veck. Performer Harold Brown, Howard Lyman, Cayce Mell, Cheri Ezell-Vandersluis, Willow Jeane Lyman, Jim Vandersluis and Jason Tracy. Tribe of Heart, 2009. DVD. 27:10 min.
32. Animal Cruelty - Dairy. Vegan Peace. http://bit.ly/1OjColv
33. Cage-Free Eggs: The Faces of Free Range, HumanMyth.org http://bit.ly/1d7DhNi
34. Don't Buy The Myth! Humanemyth.org. http://bit.ly/1JixXUz

35. A Comparison of Regulations for the Transport of Farm Animals in Canada, The United States and the European Union. Getcrackingcruelty.ca http://bit.ly/1DiAypb
36. Top 10 Reasons Not to Eat Pigs. All-Creatures.org. http://bit.ly/1EtB99u
37. Ohio Dairy Farm Brutality. Mercy for Animals, May 25, 2010. https://youtu.be/gYTkM1OHFQg
38. Humane, Oxford Dictionary. http://bit.ly/1Elhxb3
39. Humane Myth Glossary: Humane Slaughter, HumaneMyth.org. http://bit.ly/1aX1X9M
40. Duck and Geese, My Vegan Mind. http://bit.ly/1d7Kqxc
41. Antibiotic Resistance, NRDC http://on.nrdc.org/1FiXE52
42. Peaceable Kingdom: The Journey Home. Director Jenny Stein. Producer James La Veck. Performer Harold Brown, Howard Lyman, Cayce Mell, Cheri Ezell-Vandersluis, Willow Jeane Lyman, Jim Vandersluis and Jason Tracy. Tribe of Heart, 2009. DVD. 8:15 min.
43. Hamilton, Tracey. Pythagoras' Views on Female, Animal, and Plant Rights: The Path to Ecocentrism and Enlightenment. Professor Kenneth Dorter, Print
44. Leo Tolstoy at Brainy Quotes. http://bit.ly/1PsLkCj

Chapter Five – The Oceans, Our Lifeline

1. Paul Watson and Joseph Connelly, The VN Interview: Captain Paul Watson, VegNews, March–April 2003, Page 25.
2. Paul Watson Brave Guardian of the Sea, Parts 1+2. Supreme Master Television. https://youtu.be/vKiYOguoCPQ 15 min.
3. Estimate of Fish Numbers. fishcount.org.uk. http://bit.ly/1GhPgPC
4. Worm, B. Science, November 3, 2006; Volume 314: Pages 787-790.
5. Sharkwater. Director Rob Stewart. Producer Rob Stewart. Performer Rob Stewart, Captain Paul Watson. Freestyle Releasing, 2006/07. DVD.
6. Commercial Fishing, Food Empowerment Project. http://bit.ly/1HCjMHO
7. Professor Victoria Braithwaite. Pain in Fish. http://bit.ly/1Kfmx1F
8. Do Fish Feel Pain? Stop Animal Cruelty Series on Supreme Master TV. https://youtu.be/Wk7AuWkvtxE
9. Kent, Barry MacKay. Catch and Release, Animal Issues, Spring 2003. Page 20
10. Fish Exploited for Food Suffer like Mammals and Birds, Free From Harm. http://bit.ly/1DmnjUB
11. Unconscionable Cruelty Behind Meat An Interview with Dr. Jeffrey Masson. Supreme Master Television. December 11, 2010. https://youtu.be/PouONmw-q48
12. Tuttle, Will. Chapter Fourteen, Journey of Transformation. The World Peace Diet: Eating for Spiritual Health and Social Harmony. Lantern, 2005. Print. Page 257.

13. Canada's Commercial Seal Slaughter 2009. IFAW, International Fund for Animal Welfare, 2009. Web. 9 Mar. 2014. http://bit.ly/1DJK1GM
14. Seal Hunt Quotas (Total Allowable Catch, TAC) and Official Numbers of Seals Killed Over the Years. Harpseals.org http://bit.ly/1z3Uhhu
15. More Than 98 Percent of Seals Killed at Less Than Three Months of Age, Humane Society International/Canada. http://bit.ly/1zY8w2q
16. Cove Guardians. Sea Shepherd Conservation Society. http://bit.ly/1OnV8R4
17. Earthlings. Dir. Shaun Monson. Performer Joaquin Phoenix, Moby. 2005. 45:54 min.
18. Sharkwater. Director Rob Stewart. Producer Rob Stewart. Performer Rob Stewart, Captain Paul Watson. Freestyle Releasing, 2006/07. DVD.

Chapter Six – The World's Religions and Spiritual Traditions

1. Neurolove.me. http://bit.ly/1z2nWaF
2. List of Religious Populations. Wikipedia. http://bit.ly/1DpJlWD
3. Jain Vegetarianism. Wikipedia. http://bit.ly/1QwIwpk
4. Plutarch, de Esu Carn. Pages 993, 996, 997
5. Pythagoreanism. Wikipedia. http://bit.ly/1GlBJq9
6. http://bit.ly/1z9bTc0
7. http://bit.ly/1dgFfLp
8. http://bit.ly/1OULGQ1
9. History of Vegetarianism – Plutarch. International Vegetarian Union (IVU). http://bit.ly/1dgId2s
10. The Ten Commandments. The Holy Bible: King James Version. Hendrickson, 2004. Print. Page 1358.
11. Exodus 20:13. The Holy Bible: King James Version. Hendrickson, 2004. Print N. 97
12. Deuteronomy 5:17. The Holy Bible: King James Version. Hendrickson, 2004. Print. Page 245.
13. Genesis 9:4. The Holy Bible: King James Version. Hendrickson, 2004. Print. Page 10.
14. Romans 15:21. The Holy Bible: King James Version. Peabody, MA: Hendrickson, 2004. Print. Page 1359.
15. Genesis 1, American Bible Society. http://bit.ly/1J12MKk
16. Genesis 1:26. The Holy Bible: King James Version. Peabody, MA: Hendrickson, 2004. Print. Page 2.
17. Dominion. The Free Dictionary. Farlex, http://bit.ly/1PGHTYX
18. FAQ: Starter Guide. Vegan Outreach. http://bit.ly/1z9rvMA

Chapter Seven – Other Ways We Use Animals

1. Cat. Wikipedia. http://bit.ly/1J19WOB
2. Dog. Wikipedia. http://bit.ly/1EG5wyP
3. V-dog - For Pooch & Planet. http://v-dog.com
4. Amì Pet Food - The Natural Choice. www.amipetfood.com

5. Vegan Pet Food, Vegan Dog Food, Vegan Cat Food. Evolution Diet Pet Food Inc. http://petfoodshop.com
6. Dead Cats And Dogs Used To Make Pet Food, rense.com. http://bit.ly/1IcRm89
7. Animal Cruelty - Fur. Vegan Peace. http://bit.ly/1Gx45mA
8. Fur Farms, Fur Free Alliance. http://bit.ly/1J1rqua
9. Dog and Cat Fur. Fur-Bearer Defenders. http://bit.ly/1KkPycg
10. Earthlings. Director, Shaun Monson. Performer, Joaquin Phoenix, Moby. 2005. 46:24 – 51:34 min.
11. Skin Trade. Director, Shannon Keith. Uncaged Films, 2010.
12. Ibid.
13. Ibid.
14. Earthlings. Director, Shaun Monson. Performer, Joaquin Phoenix, Moby. 2005. 50:51 min.
15. Ibid. 51:13 – 51:49 min.
16. Live Plucking of Ducks for Down, http://bit.ly/1bIudOw
17. Cruel Truth of how Angora Rabbit Fur is Removed. https://youtu.be/5TmQ_t_Lf28
18. US' Investigation: Sheep Killed for Wool. https://youtu.be/eLo1KeYCjpk
19. Fast Facts: Silk, Your Daily Vegan. http://bit.ly/1FoSMvx
20. Skin Trade. Dir. Shannon Keith. Uncaged Films, 2010. DVD.
21. Carman, Judy. Chapter Two: The Awakening of Humanity to Compassion. Peace to All Beings: Veggie Soup for the Chicken's Soul. Lantern, 2003. Print. Page 45.
22. Animals Exploited for Entertainment (Circuses), OCPA. http://bit.ly/1DqD50Q
23. The Romance and Reality of Bullfighting, Encyclopædia Britannica. http://bit.ly/1bIyhyt
24. Vivisection. Wikipedia. http://bit.ly/1IcXb5j
25. Moving Beyond Animal Research, PCRM. http://bit.ly/1HL4G4r
26. Product Testing: Animal Testign Science and Facts, Vivisection Information Network. http://bit.ly/1Gw5Uxn
27. Animals and Product Testing, National Anti-Vivisection Society. http://bit.ly/1J1NPHP
28. Alternatives to Animal Testing and Research. New England Anti-Vivisection Society. http://bit.ly/1FpTjx6
29. Correspondent, Fiona Macrae Science. Food Giants Caught in Animal Testing Scandal. Mail Online. Associated Newspapers, 20 June 2013. http://dailym.ai/1Gn5NSi
30. Companies That Still Test on Animals. The Vegetarian Site. http://bit.ly/1EaITiR
31. Quote by Mark Twain. GoodReads. http://bit.ly/1A3CIsP
32. What Are Alternatives to Animal Testing? Vegetarian Times. http://bit.ly/1DAUp4A

Chapter Eight – Human Rights

1. Famous Vegans - Michael Greger. Vegan Peace. http://bit.ly/1zcjkiq
2. Why People Must Be Vegetarian. The Supreme Master Ching Hai International Association. http://bit.ly/1J2hznT
3. Meat: Now It is Not Personal! World Watch Institute, Excerpted from the July/August 2004 World Watch Magazine. http://bit.ly/1JJlDd0
4. Tuttle, Will. Chapter Three: The Nature of Intelligence. The World Peace Diet: Eating for Spiritual Health and Social Harmony. Lantern, 2005. Print. Page 37.
5. Ibid. Page 22.
6. A Case for the World Peace Diet with Vegan Author Dr. Will Tuttle. Supreme Master Television http://youtu.be/gzu9P-nwN10
7. Pimentel, David. Energy Inputs in Food Crop Production in Developing and Developed Nations. January 16, 2009. http://bit.ly/1EaLWYc
8. Pimentel, David.U.S. Could Feed 800 Million People with Grain That Livestock Eat, Cornell Ecologist Advises Animal Scientists | Cornell Chronicle. Cornell University. August 1, 1997. http://bit.ly/1DAX527
9. Tich Nhat Hanh, Eating for Peace - the Art and Science of Mindful Consumption. Earth Save. http://bit.ly/1JuwlXS
10. A Life Connected: Vegan. Nonviolence United. http://veganvideo.org
11. Tomasko, Felicia. Sitting Down With: Will Tuttle. LA Yoga Ayurveda and Health Magazine. http://bit.ly/1b5fz2H
12. Tuttle, Will M. Chapter Three: As We Sow, So Shall We Reap. The World Peace Diet: Eating for Spiritual Health and Social Harmony. Lantern, 2005. Print. Pages 46-47.
13. Eisnitz, Gail. Slaughterhouse: The Shocking Story of Greed, Neglect, and Inhumane Treatment inside the U.S. Meat Industry. Prometheus, 1997, 2007. Print.
14. Schlosser, Eric. The Chain Never Stops, Mother Jones, July-Aug. 2001. http://bit.ly/1Gnev31
15. Lance Gompa, professor of industrial and labor relations at Cornell University, lead researcher in Human Rights Watch's report Blood Sweat, and Fear: Workers' Rights in U.S. Meat and Poultry Plants, January 2005.
16. Steven Greenhouse, Human Rights Watch Report Condemns U.S. Meat Packing Industry For Violating Basic Human And Worker Rights, New York Times, January 25, 2005.
17. Eisnitz, Gail. Slaughterhouse: The Shocking Story of Greed, Neglect, and Inhumane Treatment inside the U.S. Meat Industry. Prometheus, 1997, 2007. Print. Page 62.
18. Animal: Definition of Animal in Oxford Dictionary. Oxford University Press. http://bit.ly/1JJr9MG
19. http://bit.ly/1z4c33R

Chapter Nine – Celebrities Who Live the Compassionate Life

1. Talk:List of Vegans/Temp: Disputed Cases. Wikipedia.

http://bit.ly/1OX7J8G
2. Ellen Pompeo Talks Backyard Chickens on Ellen. MNN Holdings, LLC. http://bit.ly/1J2pB06
3. Silverstone, Alicia. The Kind Diet. Rodale, 2011. Print.
4. List of Vegans. Wikipedia. http://bit.ly/1GwLYug

Chapter Ten – Why They Are not Vegan

1. Kijiji. www.kijiji.ca
2. Craigslist. www.craigslist.org
3. History of Tofu. Soya.be http://bit.ly/1bvbCor
4. The Law of Vibration. Camillo Loken. http://bit.ly/1b5lBQZ
5. Blog: Food and Vibrational Frequency. HealingThruFood. http://bit.ly/1EvBvjx
6. Extremism. Wikipedia. http://bit.ly/1zcEf50
7. Morality. Wikipedia. http://bit.ly/1HJaz0F
8. Benjamin Zephaniah | Interviews and Features | Vegetarian Living Magazine. Vegetarian Living. http://bit.ly/1zcFiBV

Chapter Eleven – Do Plants Feel Pain?

1. Plant Perception (a.k.a. the Backster Effect). The Skeptic's Dictionary. http://bit.ly/1JJu4op
2. The World Peace Diet. An Interview with Dr. Will Tuttle. Animal Advocate Inc. https://youtu.be/Zb-NzViPGnk
3. FAQ: Starter Guide. Vegan Outreach. http://bit.ly/1HJbDBA

Chapter Twelve – Love is the Answer

1. Spiritual Inspiration Quotes. The Supreme Master Ching Hai International Association. http://bit.ly/1b7OQTe
2. Peaceable Kingdom: The Journey Home. Director Jenny Stein. Producer James LaVeck. Tribe of Heart, 2009. DVD. 1hr. 12min.
3. Vegucated. Director Marisa Miller Wolfson. Kind Green Planet, 2011. DVD.
4. Halbfass, Wilhelm. Karma und Wiedergeburt im indischen Denken, Diederichs, München, Germany, 2000.
5. Lawrence C. Becker & Charlotte B. Becker, Encyclopedia of Ethics, 2nd Edition, Hindu Ethics. Page 678.
6. Peaceable Kingdom: The Journey Home. Dir. Jenny Stein. Prod. James LaVeck. Tribe of Heart, 2009. DVD. Edited quote of Harold Brown through email contact.
7. King, Martin Luther, Jr. Loving Your Enemies. Class of Nonviolence. Lesson For: Essay Two. SalsaNet. http://bit.ly/1IgMNcZ
8. Carman, Judy. Peace to All Beings: Veggie Soup for the Chicken's Soul. Lantern, 2003. 111. Print.
9. Albert Einstein, letter dated 1950, quoted in H. Eves, Mathematical Circles Adieu, 1977
10. O'Neil, Dennis. What Is Anthropology: Overview. Palomar Community College District. http://bit.ly/1OZLBKJ

11. A Very Wise Old Man Has Something to Say... Humans Are a Tropical Species. http://bit.ly/1Eg4433
12. Letter from Cesar Chavez Regarding Nonviolence Toward Animals. http://bit.ly/1z7BuBA
13. Extracts from some journals 1842-48 - the earliest known uses of the word 'vegetarian' Compiled by John Davis http://bit.ly/1DEun0k
14. Donald Watson. Wikipedia. http://bit.ly/1QCc0C4
15. Memorandum Of Association Of The Vegan Society. The Vegan Society. Page 1, clause 3. http://bit.ly/1EKVNHI
16. Lacto-ovo Vegetarians. Wikipedia. http://bit.ly/1b7UaWt
17. The Straight Dope: Is Honey Really Bee Vomit? http://bit.ly/1DvftYV
18. Prabhupada, A.C. Bhaktivedanta Swami. Why We Don't Eat Meat. Why We Dont Eat Meat. http://bit.ly/1J5dpvw
19. Cesar Chávez: A Champion of Animal Rights, IDA USA. https://youtu.be/opAhAh1dyW0
20. Anatole France. http://bit.ly/1OxaToQ
21. Charles Darwin Quotations. Archive From All-creatures.org. http://bit.ly/1zhdHzK

Chapter Thirteen – Making The Transition

1. Dalrymple, G. Brent. The age of the earth in the twentieth century: a problem (mostly) solved. Special Publications, Geological Society of London. 2001, 190 (1): Pages 205–221.
2. Manhesa, Gérard; Allègre, Claude J.; Dupréa, Bernard; and Hamelin, Bruno (1980). Lead isotope study of basic-ultrabasic layered complexes: Speculations about the age of the earth and primitive mantle characteristics. 47 (3): Pages 370–382.
3. Tuttle, Will. Chapter One: Food's Power. The World Peace Diet: Eating for Spiritual Health and Social Harmony. New York: Lantern, 2005. Print. Pages 11-12.
4. Freston, Kathy. Eating Vegan on the Cheap. The Huffington Post. TheHuffingtonPost.com 28 Mar. 2011. http://huff.to/1EL28Tn

Chapter Fourteen – Why We Must Promote Compassion

1. Farm to Fridge. Mercy for Animals. https://youtu.be/ju7-n7wygP0
2. 10 Billion Lives. FARM, Farm Animal Rights Movement. www.10billionlives.com

Chapter Fifteen – How Meat Kills us and Veganism Saves the World

1. Lin, Doris. What's Wrong with Grass-Fed Beef? About.com Animal Rights. http://abt.cm/1GVH6fX
2. Nearly Two Billion People Worldwide Now Overweight. Worldwatch Institute. June 14, 2011. http://bit.ly/1GVHhbf
3. Pimentel, David: Agriculture and Food Problems. Principles of Environmental Sciences. 2009, Pages 513 – 516. http://bit.ly/1P8DjWx

4. Global Meat Production and Consumption Continue to Rise. Worldwatch Institute. http://bit.ly/1JWNg5K
5. Global and Regional Food Consumption Patterns and Trends. World Health Organization, WHO. http://bit.ly/1ElYJot
6. Rifkin, Jeremy. Feed the World. VIVA, Guide 12, Second Edition, 2006. http://bit.ly/1Ioj4zU
7. The State of the Planet's Biodiversity. World Environment Day 2010. United Nations Environment Programme. http://bit.ly/1dU4mnB
8. The Carbon Cycle: Feature Articles. The earth Observatory: EOS Project Science Office. http://1.usa.gov/1IojGWi
9. Animal Product Consumption and Mortality Because of All Causes Combined, Coronary Heart Disease, Stroke, Diabetes, and Cancer in Seventh-day Adventists. National Center for Biotechnology Information. U.S. National Library of Medicine, Sept. 1988. Pages 739 - 748. http://1.usa.gov/1GVIPlv
10. A Delicate Balance: The Truth. Pheonix Philms, 2008. DVD.
11. Bycatch, Wikipedia. http://bit.ly/1KuYjQx
12. Paul Watson Brave Guardian of the Sea (Parts 1+2). Supreme Master Television, 11 July 2011. https://youtu.be/vKiYOguoCPQ
13. Toxins in Fish, Sea The Truth. http://bit.ly/1P8IiGz
14. Cooke, Steve. Pain and Suffering in Nonhuman Animals. http://bit.ly/1Kv0lA9
15. Humane Myth Glossary: Humane Slaughter. Humane Myth, http://bit.ly/1zT8PkA

Chapter Sixteen – Fruitarianism: The Garden of Eden

1. Wodzak, Mango. Eden Fruitarianism. Destination Eden. Lulu Press Inc., 2013. Print. Page 109.
2. Graham, Douglas. How Fruits Will Save the World: The Sweet, Simple Solution. FoodnSport. https://youtu.be/oLKKVBCE2nI
3. Graham, Douglas. Environment. Grain Damage. 2005 edition. FoodnSport: Food for Thought, 1998. Print. Page 37.
4. Wodzak, Mango. Eden Fruitarianism: Ethical Food Tower. Destination Eden. First Edition Lulu Press, 2013. Print. Page 116
5. Food Packaging and Its Environmental Impact. Food Technology Magazine April 2007. http://bit.ly/1Fc9UGa
6. Cho, Renee. What Happens to All That Plastic? – State of the Planet. State of the Planet. Earth Institute, Columbia University, January 31, 2012. http://bit.ly/1ANmC77
7. The Plastic Cow. Karuna Society for Animals and Nature, April 20, 2012. https://youtu.be/SifRIYqHfcY
8. Raw Till 4: Official Facebook Group. www.rawtill4.com

Chapter Seventeen – The Journey to Compassionate Choices

1. Dairy and Ear Infections: Is There an Association? NutritionFacts.org, November 8, 2012. http://bit.ly/1dUbfW2

2. Hertzler SR, Huynh BCL, Savaiano DA. How much lactose is low lactose? Journal of the American Dietetic Association. March 1996. Pages 243 - 246.
3. Lin, Doris. Vegans and Honey: Why Vegans Don't Eat Honey. About.com Animal Rights. http://abt.cm/1J009uk
4. Wodzak, Mango. Eden Fruitarianism: Topsy-Turvey World. Destination Eden. First Edition. Lulu Press, 2013. Print. Page 213.
5. Balcombe, Jonathan. They Think, Feel Pain. PCRM, Physicians Committee for Responsible Medicine / The Miami Herald, November 10, 2006. http://bit.ly/1FcdEre
6. Prêmio Brilhante Herói Mundial Dr. Will Tuttle – Para Os Animais, a Humanidade E a Paz Mundial. Will Tuttle on Supreme Master Television. http://bit.ly/1ANqQvB
7. Earthlings. Dir. Shaun Monson. Performer Joaquin Phoenix, Moby. Nation Earth, 2005. DVD
8. Peaceable Kingdom: The Journey Home. James LaVeck and Jenny Stein. Tribe of Heart, 2009. DVD.
9. Tuttle, Will M. The World Peace Diet: Eating for Spiritual Health and Social Harmony. Lantern, Print. 2005. Print.
10. Carman, Judy. Peace to All Beings: Veggie Soup for the Chicken's Soul. New York, Lantern, Print. 2003.
11. Labeling. CBAN, The Canadian Biotechnology Action Network, May 9, 2015. http://bit.ly/1Pq9ahV
12. Animal Ingredients and Products. The Vegan Sandwich. Last updated March 1, 2015. http://thevegansandwich.com/?p=95
13. Animal Cruelty: Dairy. Vegan Peace. http://bit.ly/1OjColv
14. Ibid.
15. Gems From the Great Health Debate with Dr. Will Tuttle and Sally Fallon. Maria's Blog - The Green Smoothie Challenge. http://bit.ly/1JzZfD9
16. The Price of Milk/Dairy - Separation of a Cow and Her Calf. France 3. https://youtu.be/SYJPbrxdn8w
17. Come from a Grieving Mother Pamphlet. Peaceful Prairie Sanctuary. http://bit.ly/1APkpbd
18. Holmberg, Marta. Are Eggs Chicken Periods? A Nurse Gives the Lowdown. Peta2.com, February 4, 2015. http://bit.ly/1Pbk7qV
19. United Poultry Concerns (UPC). www.upc-online.org
20. Davis, Karen, PhD. The Perils and Pleasures of Urban Backyard Chicken-Keeping. United Poultry Concerns [UPC]. The Sacramento Bee, March 25, 2010 Portland Press Herald (Maine), March 28, 2010. http://bit.ly/1H7VmF6
21. Davis, Karen, PhD. UPC Letter Regarding the Keeping of Chickens and Goats for Eggs and Milk in Long Beach. United Poultry Concerns, July 19, 2012. http://bit.ly/1H7VKTV
22. Ching Hai, Supreme Master. The Key of Immediate Enlightenment. Supreme Master Ching Hai Association, Print. Page 61.

23. Animal Rights: A History Leo Tolstroy. Think Differently About Sheep. http://bit.ly/1H7Xxsc
24. Carman, Judy. Peace to All Beings: Veggie Soup for the Chicken's Soul. Lantern, 2003. Print. Pages 117-118.

Chapter Eighteen – My Younger Years

1. Zoochosis: What Really Happens to Animals in Captivity. One Green Planet. http://bit.ly/1JA5AOV
2. Animal Cruelty – Zoos, Vegan Peace. http://bit.ly/1cF02bu
3. Arnau, Anna. Zoo Lifestyle Not Suitable for Animals. Technique, June 29, 2012. http://bit.ly/1zQziyT
4. Homeschooling. Wikipedia. http://bit.ly/1Eqnv72
5. Unconditional Love. Wikipedia. http://bit.ly/1PbAZ0K

Chapter Nineteen – Other Issues

1. Prevalence of Tobacco Consumption. Wikipedia. http://bit.ly/1GXMr6r
2. Harms of Smoking and Health Benefits of Quitting - National Cancer Institute. http://1.usa.gov/1JAaFGI
3. Martin, Terry. 599 Additives in Cigarettes. About.com. http://abt.cm/1EqqiNs
4. Sustainable Table: Public Health. GRACE Communications http://bit.ly/1FXMSl5
5. Benefits of Alcohol, Drug, Meat and Smoking Bans. Supreme Master Television. http://bit.ly/1EqroJe
6. Ask the Expert: Alcohol. The Physicians Committee for Responsible Medicine, PCRM. http://bit.ly/1dVMdpw
7. Barnard, Neal. So, Is Wine in the Fruit Group? Power Foods for the Brain. Hachette Book Group, 2013. PDF First Edition. Page 87.
8. Barnard, Neal. Breaking the Food Seduction. St. Martin's, Print. 2003.
9. Decaffeinated Coffee Is Not Caffeine-free, Experts Say. University of Florida/ScienceDaily, October 15, 2006. http://bit.ly/1F0cVGq
10. Caffeine." Wikipedia. http://bit.ly/1Rsb4AK
11. Erowid Caffeine Vault: Content in Beverages. http://bit.ly/1KVvFZH
12. Herbal Tea. Definition of Herbal Tea at Dictionary.com. http://bit.ly/1zUDspM
13. Veracity, Dani. The Hidden Dangers of Caffeine: How Coffee Causes Exhaustion, Fatigue and Addiction. Natural News. October 11, 2005. http://bit.ly/1cFi3Xm
14. Stomach and Duodenal Ulcers (Peptic Ulcers). Johns Hopkins Medicine. http://bit.ly/1H8hvmB
15. Skipping a Beat - the Surprise of Palpitations. The Harvard Medical School. http://bit.ly/1QzlqNH
16. Theobroma Cacao: Overview. Encyclopedia of Life. http://bit.ly/1EqABkF
17. Jeremy Safron/John Kohler. Raw Cacao/Chocolate Is Not Health Food. November 21, 2010. https://youtu.be/wArks4mczm4

18. Theobromine. Princeton University. http://bit.ly/1F7HYS0
19. Sir Ghillean Prance, Mark Nesbitt. The Cultural History of Plants. Routledge, 2004. Pages 137, 175, 178–180.
20. Theobromine Poisoning. Wikipedia. http://bit.ly/1Hbc5tU
21. Craig, Winston J.; Nguyen, Thuy T. Caffeine and theobromine levels in cocoa and carob products. Journal of Food Science, January 1984. Volume 49, Issue 1, pages 302–303, http://bit.ly/1E0TcSS
22. Children in Cocoa Production. Wikipedia. http://bit.ly/1QzsYju
23. Slavery in the Chocolate Industry. Food Empowerment Project. http://bit.ly/1bIxSef
24. Combating Child Labour In Cocoa Growing. International Programme on the Elimination of Child Labour (IPEC), February 2005. http://bit.ly/1RswgGI
25. The Dark Side of Chocolate. 2010. www.thedarksideofchocolate.org
26. Children Found Sewing Clothing For Wal-Mart, Hanes & Other U.S. & European Companies - National Labor Committee. The Labor and Worklife Program at Harvard Law School. http://bit.ly/1Is4IyB
27. Sweatshop. Wikipedia. http://bit.ly/1HbmsxZ
28. Thirteenth Amendment to the United States Constitution. Wikipedia. http://bit.ly/1dW08Mh
29. Slavery. Wikipedia. http://bit.ly/1dW0xOP
30. New Zealand Women and the Vote. History Group of the New Zealand Ministry for Culture and Heritage. https://bitly.com/a/bitlinks
31. Australian Suffragettes. Australian Government http://bit.ly/1F0vY3m
32. Woman Suffrage. National Museum of American History. Smithsonian Institution. http://bit.ly/1E1002Z
33. Women's Right to Vote in Canada. Parliament of Canada. http://bit.ly/1E10rdB
34. Women and the Vote. UK Parliament. http://bit.ly/1IuXaJY
35. The Persons Case, 1927-1929: The Famous Five. Library and Archives Canada. http://bit.ly/1HbuYgc

Afterword

1. Loving Hut. Wikipedia. http://bit.ly/1IsbUdZ

ABOUT ME

Photo by Agnes Cseke

An acclaimed author, educator and filmmaker, Michael Lanfield is a certified World Peace Diet facilitator. Inspired and taught by Dr. Will Tuttle, his talks are informative, inspiring and interactive. He is the author of the book The Interconnectedness of Life with foreword by Dr. Karen Davis, author and president of United Poultry Concerns and is currently writing and producing a documentary film under the same name based on his book. He is the founder of the non-profit organizations We Are Interconnected Films and The Vegan Sandwich.

Made in the USA
Lexington, KY
10 October 2016